ADVANCE PRAISE

"At some point, every one of your customers is going to ask, 'What is the exact value you are providing us?' And they are going to want a quantifiable answer. Rob Bernshteyn explains why that day is going to come sooner than you think. More importantly, he lays out in a step-by-step fashion how you and your company can provide value as a service."

—**William A. Sahlman,** Harvard Business School, Class of 1955
Professor of Business Administration

"Value disruption is inevitable. With global hypercompetition, sustained revenue growth is becoming more elusive. Gaining greater operational efficiencies is the new battleground where real leverage is required for every dollar spent. Bernshteyn's book offers a no-nonsense guide on how to approach this developing business dynamic."

—**Roger Siboni,** chief executive officer of Epiphany,
chief operating officer of KPMG

"Honed on the cutting edge of the software industry's ongoing transformation, *Value as a Service* is an insightful, practical, and indispensable guide to success in the new digital era of business. Rob Bernshteyn explains in masterful clarity why the winners in the as-a-service enterprise future will be those who truly engage customers in creating and sustaining measurable business value."

—**Phil Wainewright,** cofounder of Diginomica

"There is a new customer contract emerging that Rob Bernshteyn calls *value as a service*. If your business is not organized around this principle, it is at risk. At MDV and Wildcat Technology Ventures, we invest in companies that use next-generation technology to release this type of "trapped value", value that cannot be realized because it is trapped inside of legacy processes designed for a prior era. That's what customers want to buy. That's what companies like Coupa are committed to deliver."

—**Geoffrey Moore,** author of *Crossing the Chasm,*
The Gorilla Game, and *Inside the Tornado*

"Rob Bernshteyn masterfully explains in *Value as a Service* that we are going to have to move beyond providing software as a service; we must provide real value as a service, where you can quantify exactly what you are providing to your customers. At DocuSign, we utilize this concept of value proposition quantification to demonstrate to customers large and small why implementing a digital translation management system is not only critical to but should be the first step in achieving a successful digital transformation."

—**Keith Krach,** chairman and chief executive officer
of DocuSign, cofounder of Ariba

"Rob Bernshteyn's *Value as a Service* illuminates the future of business exchange: quantifiable value. Provide it and compete, or offer vague assurances, busy work, and mere customer 'satisfaction' on the road to irrelevance. Bernshteyn offers a blueprint for both companies and the individuals they employ to disrupt to a business model focused on quantifiable results that add value and drive success. No more just 'dialing it in' to do a job. An exciting prospect for today's millennials who want to bring their best ideas to the workplace. Bernshteyn's firm grasp of business realities can be yours. A lively, thought-provoking read."

—**Whitney Johnson,** Thinkers50 World's Most Influential Management Thinkers,
author of critically acclaimed *Disrupt Yourself: Putting the Power of*
Disruptive Innovation to Work

VALUE
AS A
EMBRACING
THE COMING
DISRUPTION
SERVICE

ROB BERNSHTEYN

GREENLEAF
BOOK GROUP PRESS

This publication is designed to provide accurate and authoritative information in regard to the subject matter covered. It is sold with the understanding that the publisher and author are not engaged in rendering legal, accounting, or other professional services. If legal advice or other expert assistance is required, the services of a competent professional should be sought.

Published by Greenleaf Book Group Press
Austin, Texas
www.gbgpress.com

Distributed by Greenleaf Book Group

For ordering information or special discounts for bulk purchases, please contact Greenleaf Book Group at PO Box 91869, Austin, TX 78709, 512.891.6100.

Design and composition by Greenleaf Book Group
Cover design by Greenleaf Book Group
Cover image: istock.com/©filo

Publisher's Cataloging Publication Data is available.

ISBN: 978-1-62634-305-4

Part of the Tree Neutral® program, which offsets the number of trees consumed in the production and printing of this book by taking proactive steps, such as planting trees in direct proportion to the number of trees used: www.treeneutral.com

TreeNeutral®

Printed in the United States of America on acid-free paper

16 17 18 19 20 21   10 9 8 7 6 5 4 3 2 1

First Edition

Other Edition(s):
eBook ISBN: 978-1-62634-306-1

To Kira, Tyler, and Kyle

CONTENTS

CHAPTER 1

MIDNIGHT IN PARIS: VALUE AS A SERVICE AND HOW IT CAN HELP YOU

Most people who go to Paris return with memories of wonderful meals, inspiring art and architecture, and perhaps a souvenir or two.

I went to Paris and returned to the United States with a business insight that changed my career, one that could improve yours—and the performance of your company.

Let me tell you what happened.

I was working in Paris as a consultant, implementing software for Alcatel Telecom (now Alcatel-Lucent), the huge French global telecommunications equipment conglomerate. Alcatel had recently bought tens of millions of dollars of software from SAP, a software company based in Germany. My job was to lead a team of thirteen consultants to get the software up and running and help Alcatel go live.

It was an amazing career opportunity for me. Andersen Consulting, my employer, not only paid for me to live in a beautiful apartment overlooking the Eiffel Tower but also for my flights back and forth from my place in New York whenever I wanted. In exchange, I had to get the software to work.

For those of you unfamiliar with the software industry, imagine that you (Alcatel) just bought millions of dollars' worth of furniture (the SAP software) from IKEA, but you don't know how to assemble it yourself. Your best bet is to pay your local handymen (Andersen Consulting) to assemble it correctly and quickly. Enterprise software, much like the IKEA furniture that comes unassembled in a box, is not useful until properly installed.

Although the project was progressing well, I couldn't get one nagging thought out of my head: I simply wasn't sure what value the software, which would be used to help manage Alcatel's financials, provided. I didn't understand what Alcatel was getting for their money by buying the software.

SAP had sold their software to Alcatel for tens of millions of dollars. So I understood the value created for SAP. Alcatel was paying me and my team thousands of dollars an hour for our combined time, so I understood the value created for Andersen Consulting as well. But what about our client? When I looked across the table at Alcatel's working team on the project, for the life of me, I couldn't understand what of value they would receive when our work was done. What would be the thing they could point to? That the software worked? That the information was now more centralized? That some of their employees used it? That they got a lot of transactional volume through the system? That the big boss was happy? What *exactly* would make this multimillion-dollar project a success?

The answer, we told ourselves, was that it would perhaps automate some processes, which was probably right, but that was awfully amorphous. I couldn't point to anything specific our client would be getting in return for their money.

I thought, *This kind of squishy payoff can't last forever. After all, SAP is getting paid handsomely, and so is Andersen, but what is the client getting? The world is becoming more operationally efficient. Over time, companies are going to squeeze out a lot of these inefficiencies and figure out a tangible payoff to things like installing new software, and I want to be part of the group that creates this disruption.* So I got my MBA, moved out to Silicon Valley, and began working for an enterprise software company, because I figured that was the best way to understand the industry and get closer to real quantifiable value creation.

Over the next few years, the enterprise software industry did become a bit more efficient. Instead of selling customers software that required them to hire consultants to make it work, we provided a product slightly easier to use and install over the web by way of subscription. Delivering software over the web was a better execution of the application service provider (ASP) model of the late 1980s. This time, we called it *cloud computing*. It was basically the same as what we had been doing before, but it did introduce some new efficiency. That added a bit more value, because you were getting the product via subscription; you paid as you went. You didn't have to shell out millions of dollars up front. The product became a service. And this approach allowed for sharing some of the risk. Before, you paid for the product and had to assume all the risk of making it work. But now, because you were getting it by subscription, you could cancel if you were unhappy with the way things were going.

But still, the only thing that had really changed was that the process had become more operationally efficient. The stuff was delivered pay-as-you-go, and the consultants needed to do less, because the software was easier to configure. But the focus was still on taking the customer live—getting the stuff to work.

There was still nothing of distinct value that either the software vendor or the customer could point to.

Over time, our industry as a whole made tentative steps toward a payoff. For example, we could point to increased efficiency from buying our products. The work our clients did, in some cases, got done more quickly and with fewer people as a result of what we were selling. But these were one-time savings. Yes, once the software was installed, work got completed faster. But the speed did not increase over time. And once the initial wave of people was gone, they were gone. The head count didn't go any lower. You could point to some value improvement, but that improvement didn't continue. There was no sustained improvement.

We hadn't gone to the next step, which, instead of making the process more streamlined, is delivering real value to the customer time after time, regardless of whether the product comes via the cloud or not. I was convinced that's what we needed to focus on— the actual value we delivered (i.e., the quantifiable, measurable success criteria everyone could point to). The goal should be for us to be able to say, "Because the customer bought this from us, they save X dollars a year, every year, or customer retention climbs Y percent a year, or they get to market Z days faster." Despite the small improvements, we were still far from establishing a positive correlation between buying software and tangible value creation, let alone being able to point to any real causality.

So I looked around my industry, the enterprise software industry, and asked, "Is there a place that a customer can say, 'Because I subscribe to whatever information technology solution, I have either boosted my revenue, saved a lot of money, or received something else of value in a substantial way?'" In other industries, you can easily point to those statistics. For example, because I took this express train, I got to work 40 percent faster. Because I drank this caffeinated beverage, I am 50 percent more awake. Because I used this detergent, my clothes come out 10 percent whiter than the leading brand every time.

But in our industry, I could not find that sort of statistic. This shouldn't sound surprising. Just look at the advertising from some of the most respected enterprise software companies out there. In their advertising, major companies with hundreds of millions (NetSuite) or even billions in revenue (Oracle and SAP) don't point to any offered value.

NetSuite calls itself the "platform for disruption." What does that mean?

Oracle always lists how many people use its product: "20 of the top 20 media companies." That's not value. That's peer pressure. You are not cool unless you use Oracle.

In either case, it has nothing to do with value. And SAP's ads simply say *the trendspotting cloud*. Huh?

Perhaps, not surprisingly, customers are not sure what they are getting in terms of value in our industry. Of course, that is not to say that NetSuite, Oracle, and SAP are bad companies. It simply suggests that, as an industry, we are still far from reaching the much-desired value paradigm.

WANTED: A NEW APPROACH

We need to move to a concept that I call *value as a service*. It's the simple idea that we promise that we will deliver to the customer something that will lead to quantifiable improvement: this much saved, this much improvement in lead generation, this much improvement in revenue, and this much improvement in employee retention.

> *In the future, every corporate purchaser will say, "You want me to buy what you are selling. Fine. Here's the very specific, quantifiable set of outcomes I want. Prove to me that you are going to deliver them, and I'll buy. If you can't, I won't."*

The relationship between buyer and seller should work like this. You're going to pay a subscription fee, or pay for a product or service, and in return, we will give you something of value that can be clearly and distinctly articulated.

The idea of demanding specific, quantifiable value in exchange for buying something is already firmly entrenched in mature industries (see "Look in Your Laundry Room to See the Future"). Think about something as basic as the construction industry. A supplier says, "This kind of concrete will withstand this level of load (which exceeds the maximum load in your planned structure), so we price it at X dollars." When you buy the concrete, you know exactly the value it provides. There's no room for vagueness. There's no room for marketing speak, like the concrete is "the platform for disruption." It's simply, "These are the results it will provide for you."

That hasn't happened in software yet, and that is understandable. We only reach that point when an industry has been around for a while.

Let's take the automotive industry as an example of why the age of the business sector is so important. The car industry's first iteration is probably best remembered through the famous Henry Ford quote about the Model T he was selling. He said, "You can have it in any color you want, as long as it's black." What he meant was, "We've got four wheels and a seat, and we're going to get you from point A to B, and that's all you get."

The second iteration, which occurred a few decades later, had elements of personalization: different colors, different engines and speeds, different models of the same car, that sort of thing.

The third iteration, which started a few years ago, is transportation as a service. Examples are Uber, Lyft, and Zipcar. The value received is clear. I need to get from point A to point B with a certain level of convenience, at a certain price point, and with a certain level of consistency, but I don't need to own the automobile itself. Uber, Lyft, and Zipcar deliver exactly what I want when I want it. I know exactly the value I am getting for every dollar I spend. And there are two huge potential advantages I get as a result. The first is that I no longer have to own a car. That is great news for many of us, because several studies show that our cars, on average, are used only one hour a day,[1] which means they have a paltry 4 percent use rate. What a waste. The second advantage is

---

1   http://www.racfoundation.org/research/mobility/spaced-out-perspectives-on-parking.

that I no longer have to pay a large sum of money up front (i.e., buying a car) to get this value.

Let me tie this discussion back to my software industry. In the late 1990s, the first iteration created a lot of products, and we had the world believing that technology was a huge competitive advantage for everyone, and every company should adopt it as soon as possible or risk being left behind. This thinking led, in part, to the tech bubble of the early 2000s. People bought a lot of things because other people were buying them, saying to themselves, "I can't afford to be left behind."

This phase created a lot of failures—some successes, sure, but many more failures. A lot of projects never worked. A lot of technology was deployed for the sake of deployment, without real clarity around what was produced or why it mattered to businesses. This was truly the era of the vendor, where we told customers that technology solutions would solve all their problems. If they had the money, customers could have any color they wanted, as long as it was black and they were willing to pay a lot of money up front.

The second iteration, and I'm sticking to business applications now, was the subscription idea, where you don't have to lay out all this money up front. You pay as you go. But you're still pretty much looking at the offering from the same kind of vantage point you were in the first iteration. You're saying, "Well, I'm implementing some stuff and modernizing my technology, and hopefully it gives me some sort of advantage, but I am not exactly sure what I am going to get." That's where we are now. Customers have more options. In addition to desktop software, there is now cloud-based software delivered through a web browser, for example. But none of that has been the ultimate game changer.

And the third iteration—like is happening with cars—is going to be the final frontier: *value as a service*. The first frontier is the product where nothing existed before. The second frontier presents options like a new delivery medium. The third frontier is (or in our case will be) specific, quantifiable value.

Go back to Uber. They're worth somewhere north of $50 billion as I write this. But the reason for that, some believe, is because they will be going beyond the taxi business. They're planning on delivering goods and services to your house. You want a bottle of gin? They'll get it to you within three hours through their car network. If they do that, they would no longer be only auto transportation. What would they be offering? Convenience as a service, perhaps. That is another example of where the next value frontier is going to be.

Or take medical drugs, for example. For treating headaches, the first iteration was aspirin. The second iteration got more advanced, and we got Tylenol—or the generic version, acetaminophen—which works better on headaches, and Advil, which is best for things like a swollen ankle. And from there, we have gone further, to such things as Tylenol PM, Tylenol gel caps, and all the other variations.

The third iteration? Well, there are seven billion people on the earth today, and we each have our own distinct DNA. There will be a customized, on-demand headache solution for each one of us based on our genetic background and our physical tolerance levels. It will be like this: "I want my type of headache gone within thirty seconds with almost no side effects via whatever form (pill, inhaler, drink, etc.) I prefer at that moment." We are moving rapidly to this level of custom value creation for the consumer in not just health care and transportation but in almost every single industry that influences how we live.

Again, because our industry is not mature, we haven't gotten to the point yet of providing value as a service, but we will.

Look in Your Laundry Room to See the Future

It is the nature of the beast. The longer an industry has been around, the better the (surviving) companies within it are at offering value as a service.

This comes about out of necessity. If companies in mature industries don't continuously offer more and better value, someone else will—and those that don't will cease to exist.

Take laundry detergent, which has been around for about a hundred years. (Before that, people used soap flakes to wash their clothes.) Now, it's offered in countless ways that provide value: by size—you can buy packages small enough to be approved by the TSA to carry on in your luggage when you get in a plane, or as large as thirty-two-pound boxes, which contain enough for two hundred loads; by method of delivery—you can pour it into your machine in liquid or powder form or simply drop in a capsule that is premeasured; and by function—detergent comes with every conceivable additive (it can whiten your clothes, protect colors, make your wash smell fresh, etc.).

Eventually, every company will need to offer value in every imaginable form, like detergent companies do.

Forward-thinking companies view their product portfolios in terms of value drivers and how they can provide value as a service. Value-based thinking drives innovation, which drives sustainable profits, which results in durable companies.

Are there factors other than maturity that have kept us from value-based thinking? Sure. For example, there a lot of people buying from us, and every one of them has their own value drivers. One person wants to save their company money. Another wants to do everything that she can to get promoted. So you have to be smart enough to map your primary value drivers to meet the needs of your market. (We will talk more about this in the next chapter.) But the biggest factor is the maturity of the industry.

WHY SHOULD YOU BELIEVE ME?

At this point, you might be wondering if I have tried to put all these ideas into practice at my company, Coupa, a cloud-based, spend-management software firm located in San Mateo, California, just outside of San Francisco.

The answer is yes. We most certainly have begun to put these ideas into practice.

To explain how, let me spend a minute talking about what we do.

As any company grows and gets to a certain size, it realizes that it is spending a lot of money on stuff. Somewhere along the way, the CEO, CFO, or somebody says, "Hey, we tend to buy a lot of water bottles. We're buying a lot of computers. We buy a lot of phones. How come we're paying nearly retail for everything? Why doesn't someone internally, like Bobby, negotiate with the people we do business with so that every time we buy fifty phones in bulk (for example) we get a better deal?" And that's one of the ways, you could argue, procurement came to be. Somebody was put in charge of procuring things at better prices, and they did a great job. They ended up negotiating contracts with suppliers for everything you could possibly imagine.

Baseball Cards, Bubble Gum, and
the Best Value as a Service Possible

Looking back, I realize that I was trying to provide value as a service even when I was a teenager.

When I was fourteen, I had a paper route, delivering (New York) *Newsday*. With some of the money I earned, I bought baseball cards, the ones that came inside bubble gum packs. I traded these cards with my friends, and I'd also go to collector shows.

At the shows, I noticed the guys selling cards were a lot older and moved a lot slower. You could buy a card from them for ten dollars, but if you sold it back, they would give you five dollars and then sell it again for ten dollars. There was plenty of margin, but no hustle or focus on their part. They all waited for customers to come to them.

I called up a friend of mine and said, "I bet we can beat these guys at their own game. Let's starting selling baseball cards." We pooled our collections, which totaled close to 100,000 cards, got a tax ID so we could have a table at the shows, and we were in business.

We sold a lot at our first show because we were willing to sell for less. (Clearly, one way of providing value.) Our margins were lower, but our volume made up for it. My friend and I probably split $600 in profit our first day. Our core competency—although there isn't a teenager alive who would use that term—was knowing what people wanted: hustle and ingenuity. Let me give you two quick illustrations.

We followed baseball and would get to the trade shows at seven a.m., before they opened to the public, and we walked the dealer tables as our competitors were setting up. We'd buy up all the cards of the players that had done exceptionally well that week or the rookies that were coming up who were getting a lot of press. And then, the show would open, and guess what? We were the only ones who had the hot cards—and we charged a premium for them. Offering access to a relatively scarce and desirable commodity is definitely a way of providing value as a service.

So is providing convenience. For example, we knew that collectors love to have every version of a rookie card of a potential star. We'd find the rookie card of player X that was offered by the three card companies of the time—Fleer, Topps, and Donruss. Instead of getting $8 for each individual card, we would put them in sets of three (one from each company) and charge $29. People were willing to pay a premium because we did the legwork for them (value again).

The moral? To be successful, you must create tangible value that someone is willing to pay for. It's obvious. Even a fourteen-year-old could figure it out.

But as the organizations got larger, employees didn't necessarily buy against those negotiated deals. They wound up doing what's commonly called *maverick spending*. Employees went out and bought things as they needed them, paying whatever the supplier charged, instead of the central negotiated price.

To show how this plays out, let's use a real example, a big financial services company who is a Coupa customer. They've got offices everywhere, and even though they have negotiated a nationwide bottled water contract, the executive assistant in the Des Moines office, for example, buys a couple of cases every time they need water, even though if she ordered against the corporate contract, they could have saved twenty-five cents a bottle. (We will talk about why this occurs in a minute.) This is the sort of thing that happens all the time.

So we thought, *Well, what if we can enable these people to buy against these centralized contracts through a technology platform?* If we did that, we would be offering not just another piece of software with questionable efficacy but a service that provides real value— saving money on every purchase. And that is exactly what we did, and that financial services company is now saving $100,000 a year on bottled water in the US alone. So what is the value we are providing? The value is greater savings and, therefore, greater profitability for our customer.

Before, maybe the assistant didn't know about the negotiated contract. No one had told her. Or maybe she forgot. Or maybe it wasn't convenient enough to order against it. Or perhaps she didn't have the ordering software set up in front of her in the form of a simple and easy-to-use cloud application. She wasn't being malicious; maverick spending was just more convenient for her, or she was unaware. Now, she knows about the contracts, and our product is easy to use. The bottom line: The company saves a lot of money.

Too often, with the best of intentions, centralized procurement tries to push these old, arcane technological solutions for people to use. But they're so difficult to work with and hard to access that people avoid them. At Coupa we turned the model around and made it easier for users. We worked hard to make purchasing or ordering through our system easier than any other alternative means of getting the goods or service. Once we did, we clearly realized that what we're offering is savings as a service. We're not really selling technology (although we are). We're not offering implementation (although we are). We are offering Savings as a Service, at a minimum.

It's *Product as a Service* as Well

I keep saying the central argument of this book is value as a service. But I could have easily said it is value as a product, because the makers of products are going to have to take the same approach.

Consider something as familiar as a barbecue grill. What value can that product deliver? One could be the quality of the food that's being cooked. It won't burn. The grill will slow cook the meat or chicken to keep the juices in. The value is a higher likelihood of better-tasting food.

Another value driver might be speed. An infrared grill has superfast heating. The cooking time is far faster than using charcoal or propane.

Whether you are a product or a service company, you need to point to the value you provide. That is the ultimate competitive playing field.

Once we realized that, we changed our approach to selling. We said, "Why don't we go to every customer, and instead of selling them our software, why don't we ask, 'What is your corporate spend, and how much of that do you think you can save?'"

Let's suppose they said, "We want to keep corporate spending to $300 million, and we are probably 20 percent over that."

Our response to that would be, "That's important to know. Okay, the opportunity is for $60 million in total savings."

From there, we would ask, "Where are people not adopting your procedures? Where are you having trouble?"

Once we knew that, we would say something like, "Why don't

we agree that the goal of this project is to try to save you at least $30 million a year through our system? It would be lovely to save all $60 million, but let's start with half that. That's what we are doing together. You're going to bring your expertise and people. We're going to bring our technology and best practices, and together we are going to create value. The value is reducing your spending by millions of dollars, decreasing your expenses, and increasing your profits. That's what you will be paying us to provide."

But value can take other forms beyond simply saving money. For example, some companies use our product to make sure they are in compliance with corporate policies and government regulations, so what we are also offering is compliance as a service. That's value for them. They want to make sure they have systems with approvals in place when, for example, the auditors check to see who has the right to spend a thousand dollars on dinner.

Other people value visibility. By tracking their spending, we can show them places they are going over budget, so they can take steps to get that into line. We are offering Visibility as a Service.

THIS IS EXACTLY THE SAME THING WE DO IN OUR PERSONAL LIVES

To see why value as a service is the future, you probably don't have to look much further than your personal life. Take the airline industry, for example. I try to fly Virgin America if I can.

Why? Well, the airline industry is hypercompetitive, and flights leaving at the same time for the same popular destinations are usually priced about the same. So there is no real value differentiation there. The airlines concede as much by code sharing, which is when two or more airlines share the same flight. Each airline publishes and markets the flight under its own name. And they all have basically the same frequent-flyer program—with the equally annoying inability to get the free flights you want—so there is little competitive advantage there either. And the space between the seats is about the same.

But Virgin has figured out ways to create all kinds of value as a service. It starts when you get on the plane. There is low lighting and what sounds like lounge music playing as you board. Getting on a plane and trying to get your stuff to fit in the space provided is annoying and stressful for most people. I guarantee you the lighting and the lounge music playing in the background as you board a Virgin flight lowers an average traveler's blood pressure by a measurable percentage. Virgin has created value during the half hour it takes to get everyone on board.

Then there's Virgin's safety video. Instead of annoying you with information that you already know, like how to buckle your seat belt, they have turned it into an interesting and fun music video.

The upshot of all this? They've removed the pain of boarding and created a new value driver—entertainment—during a time when you are typically the least entertained.

One more thing. You can order the type of food and the type of drinks you want from the technology display on the back of the seat in front of you. It shows you what's available, you put what you want in your digital shopping cart, and the flight attendant brings it to you. The attendants don't push a cart up and down the aisles, and you don't have to wait to see if they have what you want or not—another example of value as a service.

Let me give you one more personal example that many people can relate to—Starbucks. What are you getting there? Lot of things.

There is quality as a service, because the coffee beans they use are high quality. And then there is consistency as a service, in that you know the coffee will be relatively the same no matter what Starbucks you go to, and there is consistency in terms of how hot the coffee is and how much caffeine it contains. They have provided value, compared with their competition, around these things.

Starbucks has even figured out how to provide value with the sleeve they put around your coffee cup. If you order a certain kind of drink, one of their high-end ones, you get a sleeve of a different color. It's almost like a status symbol, similar to wearing a Hermes tie or writing with a Montblanc pen. The message the sleeve is sending to the people who notice is this: "This guy just paid seven bucks for this cup of coffee. Man, he must be somebody."

With Starbucks, you are getting a range of options. You are getting consistency. You're getting the bump in your step through the caffeine. They've broken out all the value drivers and have been able to win in a market where there are a lot of coffee shops. A key difference is that those other coffee shops didn't know how to deliver value on a consistent basis.

You might have thought that Starbucks was delivering a cup of coffee, but they are providing value as a service in many different ways (quality, consistency, status, etc.) in every cup.

WHY IS THIS IMPORTANT TO YOU?

So why should you care about all this?

Well, first, value as a service is the language you should consider speaking with others in your company. And you should consider speaking it with your vendors and demanding it in every interaction.

It's the lens through which I would argue you ought to be looking at business—and even your career.

As an employee, you don't have to necessarily change what you're doing, but you should be asking questions such as, "How is the next initiative I am going to be involved with going to be adding specific value? What distinct, quantifiable value will it deliver? How will I measure success?"

If you are purchasing products for the company, what is the quantifiable return you are getting from your purchase? How, exactly, will your company be specifically better as a result?

Eventually, if you don't start asking questions like this, you will get fired. That may sound harsh, but consider the following: You draw a regular paycheck, and your company expects that you will create much more value than you are capturing through your paycheck. If your work isn't adding tangible value, people will start asking, "Why exactly are you working on this if you can't point to a specific benefit that is going to come from it?" In a tough workplace environment, people will certainly wonder how you are helping the company.

> *In the Industrial Revolution, organizations needed bodies. Today, they need brains. One way you can prove you have the smarts that companies need is by insisting value as a service be a part of everything you are involved with.*

The flip side of that is if you concentrate on doing things that add tangible value every time, you are guaranteed to help your company do well, and you are likely going to advance and get repeatedly promoted.

TAKEAWAYS

- ▶ You should know what you are getting for your money. If you can't point to a specific return, something is wrong.

- ▶ Value can take many forms. A return does not necessarily have to be measured in dollars, but it needs to be something explicit you can point to.

- ▶ Value as a service is where the market is heading. It is going to be commonplace in years ahead, as customers across industries demand it.

WHAT'S AHEAD?

In the next chapter, we will discuss who gets to decide what value is and how it should be delivered.

CHAPTER 2

SO, WHAT EXACTLY IS VALUE? (AND WHO DETERMINES WHAT IT IS)

If we are going to spend the rest of our time talking about how you need to make value as a service a reality, it makes sense to talk about what value is and who gets to define it.

Both are important, because it turns out most of us define value incorrectly—or at least incompletely. And perhaps even worse, we let the wrong people decide what it is. (We will talk about this in detail later in the chapter, but I'll give you a hint: If you are solely letting customers define value, something is terribly wrong.)

Let's take these issues one at a time, beginning with the way value is traditionally defined. The dictionary says it's "the regard that something is held to deserve; the importance, worth, or usefulness of something." That seems clear enough.

And if you look in your old economics textbook, you will find a definition that reads something like this: "Value is a measure of the benefit provided by a good or service to someone. It is generally measured relative to units of currency, and the interpretation is therefore what is the maximum amount of money a specific actor is willing and able to pay for the good or service."

That's a bit academic-y, but it is understandable as well.

On one level, both of these definitions are fine. They certainly go substantially beyond the way some people define value, which is receiving a discount of some kind. As in, "I redeemed a valuable coupon: A box of Tide normally goes for $10, but the coupon took 25 percent off, so I only paid $7.50." Offering people a good or service at a discount is certainly one type of value creation, but it is not the only one. The world of value is much broader, so I am glad the definitions above go beyond that.

But the textbook and dictionary definitions present multiple problems, all of which can be summed up with the punch line to an old joke: "The operation was a success, but the patient died." As the punch line makes clear, it is easy to convince yourself you're creating value when you're really not.

Let's look at some situations where the existing definitions of value fail us:

- ▶ You completed a project well before the deadline. Did you deliver value? Well, if the project shouldn't have been undertaken in the first place, or if the work that was delivered was shoddy, value wasn't provided.

- ▶ You delivered a project for a client under budget. You could say you delivered value, because you saved the client some

22

money. But what are those cost savings good for (i.e., where's the value) if they don't help the client perform better?

▸ You chose the lowest-cost software solution for your company. Okay, you could argue that you got value because it was less expensive, *à la* our Tide coupon example. But maybe the software doesn't deliver any value on its own, or it takes too long to deploy, or it is too complex to configure. If any of these things are true, what value did you provide?

▸ You could be proud of yourself for giving your client a product or service that functions exactly as you promised, but if it is too complicated for anyone to use or it doesn't help the client's life in any significant way, you haven't provided any real value in the way we traditionally use the word.

▸ Someone tells you, "We got good value because we negotiated a fixed price, so our costs will be controlled." Again, so what? Your costs are controlled, but the value you receive from that contract may not be nearly as much as what you could have gotten from a contract that wasn't fixed.

All five of these examples would qualify as providing value, given the way the dictionary and professors define it. In each example, you have a "measure of benefit provided." But in reality, it is possible that nothing of value was created.

You have to know what you are measuring. It's easy to get caught up in thinking that you're creating value when all you're doing is moving the ball backward or sideways but not necessarily in the right direction.

WANTED: A NEW DEFINITION OF VALUE

We need a new description of value to make sure we are moving in the right direction. But, as I hinted at before, we also need to change who gets to define value.

Intuitively, you understand that you cannot truly define value for the customer on your own. You simply don't know their business as well as they do, and you are likely to make inaccurate assumptions about what will provide value for their business.

However, letting the customer exclusively define value isn't the correct path to follow either. For one thing, they may not have a complete handle on what they—or their customers—need.

The biggest problem caused by leaving the definition of value completely up to the customer is summed up in a quote attributed to Henry Ford, the founder of the Ford Motor Company, whom we mentioned in chapter 1. He said, "If I had asked customers what they had wanted, they would have said faster horses."

The Customer Satisfaction Myth

Every time I argue that you can't let your customers define value on their own, I get pushback that sounds like this: "How can you say that? The whole idea behind the saying *the customer is always right* is that you must satisfy the customer. If they say they have a need, you must satisfy it; that is, you need to create a product or service to fulfill it. If they say value for them is *X*, you need to do whatever it takes to give them *X*."

Well, no.

At our company, we have absolutely no interest in satisfying customers, and any company that hopes to survive today shouldn't keep

---

wasting money on trying to satisfy them either. Customer satisfaction should only be a by-product.

Let's consider a scenario you have probably sat through dozens of times, and you will understand why. You're meeting with a client group for their kickoff meeting, trying to pin down exactly what work you are going to do for them. Almost everyone in the room has a different idea of what a successful outcome would look like.

"Oh, we need to be quick."

"Oh, we need to make sure that we handle all the compliance stuff."

"Oh, we need to save money or save as much money as possible."

Or

"We need to get as much adoption as possible."

"We need to have as much end-user delight as possible."

Or

"Well, if we don't have this one feature, it's a showstopper."

Invariably (and predictably), the vendor decides to include most of everyone's wish list in an attempt to satisfy the group, and that's ultimately not helpful.

The problem with satisfaction—as in, you must always do exactly what customers say they want when they want it—is that you are constantly trying to cater to all the client group's different shifting appetites at once, rather than targeting the company's ultimate goals. It's the corporate equivalent of walking into an archery contest with one arrow in your quiver only to discover that you have to hit a dozen bull's-eyes that are moving in random directions. Good luck.

Instead of trying to satisfy everyone's wish list, you need to concentrate on delivering what will make the customer—and their company—successful.

continued on next page

> Our focus is our customers' success. At the end of the day, if your customers are successful, they will also be satisfied. But satisfaction is not success. In today's business environment, and certainly in tomorrow's, mistaking one for the other can be fatal.

Ford's point is that when it comes to innovation, customers invariably anchor on what they know. In our business, we have found that to be true. Not only is it sometimes difficult for customers to grasp new ways of doing things, but they are also tempted to hold onto the past, even when it doesn't make much sense. For example, we have had customers insist we include work-around solutions they have created to solve previous problems in their processes, even though the new approach we are proposing eliminates the original problem entirely.

Or a customer might say, for example, "We need a supplier management system, and it has to be able to do X, Y, and Z, because that's the way we've always done it in our company." But this might be automating a set of convoluted processes that are too cumbersome for anybody. In other words, the work shouldn't have been done that way to begin with.

Left to figure out what they need on their own, clients often treat enterprise software companies as they did their own information technology departments back in the early days of IT.

When IT departments started, they didn't have their own specific agendas or charters. They basically served the ad hoc needs of the business as they emerged. Someone would say, "We need laptops, and we need some systems and some software too," and IT provided whatever the business needed.

But the whole concept of enterprise software is about finding the commonalities in the ways that different companies do things, creating best practices, and encoding those practices in the most usable, flexible, and intuitive way, so they get adopted and drive results. One company can learn from both the successes and mistakes of another by implementing the best approaches in their industry. However, when customers are left to define value on their own, that doesn't happen.

However, our industry's biggest problem with letting customers completely define value is that the customer is usually not a technology firm. They are experts in construction, hospitality, health care, retail, and so on. And if the vendor is not approaching it from the customer's perspective (see "How Do You Know What Will Create Value?"), the customer is left to try to articulate what they are looking for. In that sort of situation, the customer ends up designing technology—something they are not the best equipped to do.

The way customers previously defined value in our industry, particularly in the late nineties, was by the number of features the software provided. More features meant more value. So customers started dreaming up all different kinds of features, and they started writing requests for proposals (RFPs) with hundreds of different line items for features. And vendors, in many cases, started dancing to that tune by building all these elements only to realize later—as did the customer—that the vast majority of these features were never used by anyone.

What was discovered in enterprise software, and in consumer technology as well, is that it's not about how many features the software has. Instead, it's about the features that get used and how elegantly they're built, meaning they get adopted and deployed, and people get business value out of them.

WHERE WE ARE

What we have seen is that it doesn't make sense for the supplier or the vendor to define value on their own, and having clients completely define value by themselves doesn't make sense either.

Given all this, we are back to this question: What is value, and who should define what it is? Here's where we come out: **Value is what the vendor and the customer say it is, together.** Value needs to be described, defined, and created collaboratively. And it must begin with the end goal in mind: "Here's what we are going to accomplish together." Both parties have to agree to the journey they are going on. Here's a simple analogy: If you want to go to Hawaii, and your partner says they won't go anywhere but Disneyworld, which is in Florida, you may not want to book the plane tickets yet. First, you need to align.

Value is not determined by either party alone; it comes about through the alignment of the vendor and the prospective customer. That agreement needs to be in place even before either side begins to evaluate whether they want to work with the other. Before you can decide to work together, you need to know what you are going to work together on.

We have been using business-to-business examples to show how this alignment could work, but obviously it can work in a business-to-consumer context as well. Take Enterprise Rent-A-Car, for example.

A Value Tool: Benchmarking

One way for customers and vendors to agree on a definition of value is by benchmarking. Benchmarking, in this context, is simply making a comparison between your intended goals or performance metrics and where you, or your competitors, are now. Benchmarking helps you avoid the problem of having a goal that sounds specific but really isn't. An example is if you say, "We are going to create the longest-lasting tire."

When you say "longest lasting," is it in time (years?) before the tire starts to degrade or miles driven? Or is it some combination of both? If the definition includes miles driven, under what conditions? Stop-and-go driving? Highway? Both? In what environment? Snow? Heat? All weather?

In this example, to create specificity so that you can have an agreed-upon definition of value, you would benchmark how long a tire typically lasts in various conditions, and then you would create a definition of value that might sound like this: "We are going to create a tire that runs for fifteen thousand more miles than the average tire when driven in tropical environments."

This is an unambiguous statement of value.

Here was the situation from Enterprise's perspective: They were looking for a way to rent out cars. The obvious place to set up shop was at airports, but that is exactly the place where you face competition from other car rental companies, such as Alamo, Avis, Budget, Dollar, Hertz, National, Payless, and Thrifty. Because of all that competition, you can't make a lot of money.

Here was the situation from the consumers' perspective: Some of them were looking to rent a car when theirs was being repaired, and it's not usually convenient to travel to the airport when they needed to rent one.

The solution? Enterprise would open rental offices in town—often near repair shops—and drive the rental car to the stranded customer. Enterprise created an offering that was in alignment with the customer's need for value—getting them a car when they were without one, in a minimum amount of time. In this case, Enterprise understood the customer's challenge, correctly identified that they could provide *convenience as a service* to the customer at a time of great need, and they ended up capturing tremendous value and leaving their competition in the dust (or at the airport).

> *It is impossible to satisfy everyone. Don't even try.*
> *Get people aligned around common goals.*

As we said in chapter 1, you typically find extremely close alignment in consumer industries that have been around for a while (like the rental car industry that began in 1916). Companies in mature industries need to provide value as a service, or they will be replaced by those that will.

The success of Enterprise Rent-A-Car shows what happens when a company aligns with value. The disastrous rollout of the Affordable Care Act website shows what happens when you don't.

The work done to implement the Affordable Care Act, which some people refer to as Obamacare, in the United States was one of the biggest technology website development projects ever undertaken, and everyone—regardless of their political affiliation—agrees that it was a complete mess when it launched. Why? Because there had been no agreed-upon success criteria governing the creation and launch of the website.

What was the value they were trying to generate and by when? Was it simply to have a website up and running more than 99 percent of the time? Was it to have a certain number of people enrolled by a certain date? Was it to have all the health insurance options available for consumers to easily find? Was it all of the above (and perhaps a few things more)?

As you listened to the interviews of those involved, once the website was finally live, you could hear there was no clarity about what the specific goals and value drivers were supposed to be. There was no easy way to gauge what success was. People simply weren't aligned.

That could have been because there was no agreement on what the goal was beforehand. Or it could have been because everyone involved had their own goal in mind. The consultant's value could have been creating a backend platform that got up and running. The guy from the Department of Health and Human Services might have been solely focused on ensuring enrollment forms were available. For the person in charge of the help line, it might have been that the phone number was easily accessible on the site. Everyone might have had their own individual goals, but that was not particularly helpful. There wasn't a clear way everyone could measure the overall success of the project. There were no agreed-upon criteria. Without a clear way everyone could measure the overall success of the project, there was never any real chance of a hassle-free rollout.

Consultants were often involved only for their own benefit, and

31

there were federal employees involved strictly for personal glory. The website fell on its face; it didn't work. What could be more embarrassing to the most powerful person on the planet than launching his number-one priority and having it fall on its face right out of the box due to something as simple as website scaling?

After the site finally worked, people talked all day long about how difficult it was to create this kind of website. But everyone in the software industry knew that it was not as difficult as the people involved made it look. The problem was with the lack of alignment that needed to be created for the project to succeed. (By the way, my company was guilty of exactly this sort of thing when we worked with Subway, the sandwich shop chain. I will give you all the [painful] details in chapter 4, so you can avoid the mistakes we made.)

> *If you don't know exactly what success is going to look like when you're finished, don't start.*

You need to have alignment around measurable outcomes and how value is going to be delivered before you begin. You start with the end goal in mind and work backward from there. In the case of the health care website, they could have said, "Our goal is for 95 percent of the people who don't have health insurance to sign up and for everyone who enrolls to save 3 to 5 percent on their health care costs compared with what they paid the year before, and we will set milestone targets to demonstrate value creation along the way." That's measurable and achievable, and it specifies a clear destination for everyone involved.

Once they had set the goal, they could have asked, "Who is in charge of getting people to sign up? How will they do it? What are the interim enrollment goals? How many people do we need to sign up in the first three months or in the first six months? Are there other options we might offer, such as enrolling by phone?" And they could have done the same thing for cost savings. "Who is in charge of what plans we will offer? Who is in charge of the pricing?" And so on. You have to be clear and specific.

The lack of clarity around a detailed, specific description of potential success is far from rare, as people at my company have learned repeatedly. We go into meetings all the time where potential customers spend a lot of time grilling us. As you sit across the table from them, you can almost see them thinking, *Hey, we are doing a great job of determining the scope of this project and whether these guys at Coupa are the right ones for us to partner with. They just completed our sixty-page RFP. Now we're going to sit down, and we're going to judge them.*

Then, after they have asked us a million questions (How stable is your company? Do you have enough resources? Is your technology scalable? How are you going to handle customer service?), they sit back in their chair and say, "So, do you have any questions for us?"

Invariably, we say, "Yes, we've got a question. We're sitting here one year from now, 250 business days, and we are meeting to evaluate how well the project has gone. How are we going to evaluate whether we have produced something that has mattered to anyone? How will we know that we have achieved something of value to your company?"

Nine times out of ten, they give us a blank look. They honestly haven't thought about the answer to what exactly will produce value.

They are so caught up in the process that they lose sight of delineating a goal. They book the flight tickets before they agree on the destination. It happens all the time.

That's why you have to help customers define what value is—specific, tangible, measurable value.

If you need a role model, take a look at established consumer products companies, such as Weight Watchers. They are clear and specific about what success looks like for a customer—losing weight. It is not about eating healthier, although they suggest you do. It is not about your quality of life, although that will probably improve once you lose the weight. No, the end goal is clear: Sign up with us and follow our program, and you will take the pounds off.

Now, sometimes you get lucky. You create your product or service, in conjunction with your customer, and then other people relate to it in a way you never imagined. You see this a lot in clothing companies. Patagonia set out to make outerwear for people who planned to climb Mount Kilimanjaro. But, it turned out, the average guy who only went for a walk once a week bought their clothing because he wanted to look cool. All of a sudden, Patagonia is a fashion item.

Or take Pandora, for example. As it says on its website: "At Pandora, we have a single mission: To play only music you'll love." If you are not familiar with the service, here is an oversimplified description of how it works.

You type in the title to a song you like—say, "Yesterday," by the Beatles. The company's algorithms analyze hundreds of musical details about it—melody, harmony, instrumentation, rhythm, vocals, lyrics—and then the website starts playing songs similar to "Yesterday." It becomes the seed of one of the channels you can create, and you can have up to one hundred channels.

Success, for Pandora, is offering music that people like. And many people engage with the website this way. But some people create channels to alter their mood—upbeat music when they're running or mellow music at night. Others use it as a historical source—"I want to hear every note Eric Clapton ever played." Still others use the service to see how one artist influenced another. (You can hear a lot of Bing Crosby in Frank Sinatra's music; Buck Owens affected everyone from the Eagles and Linda Ronstadt to Brad Paisley.)

How Do You Know What Is Going to Create Value?

You can ask customers what they want, but as we have seen, they don't always know. Or you can talk to your customer's customers, but they, too, could have limited perceptions of what success looks like for them. For example, in the 1950s, if you had asked people what they thought could be improved at a casual restaurant, they probably would have said they wanted a bigger burger or a smaller one or one that was served faster. They never would have described what we now know as McDonald's or included the consistency and predictability that is the hallmark of the massive restaurant chain.

So, how do you figure out what your customers may find valuable? One approach, which is particularly effective, is putting yourself in your customer's shoes.

Here's a fun example: Take a look at a regular screwdriver versus a Phillips head. The regular screwdriver came out first; craftsmen worldwide used it for decades. Sure, it slipped every once in a while, but they didn't think anything of it. They didn't stop and say, "There

continued on next page

must be a better way." They just said the thing occasionally slips, and they kept on using it.

Now, if I'm a welder or somebody who works with metals, and I put myself in the craftsmen's shoes, and I start screwing things in and the screwdriver slips every once in a while, I might say to myself, "That's really annoying. You know what? If I put a tiny *x* at the end of the tip, instead of keeping it as a flat blade that looks like a lowercase *L*, it won't slip anymore, and I bet that would make the craftsmen happy."

Looking back on it, the creation of the Phillips head screwdriver was inevitable, but the craftsmen using the regular screwdriver couldn't see it. It took someone from the outside putting themselves in the craftsmen's shoes to solve the problem.

Here's another fun example: Ever wonder why baggage claim at airports is so far away from the gate where your plane just landed? It's because value isn't always what you think it is.

Let me explain. A few years ago, officials at George Bush Intercontinental Airport in Houston, Texas, found themselves staring at an excessive number of customer complaints about the horrible wait times at baggage claim. These officials responded by adding more baggage handlers. Wait times dropped significantly, but the complaints didn't.

Undeterred, the officials conducted a deeper analysis and discovered that passengers traveled from their arrival gates to baggage claim in a minute, but then they spent seven more minutes waiting around for their bags. Armed with this data, the airport staff tried something different. They simply moved the arrival gates farther away from baggage claim, making the passengers walk longer to get to their bags. Complaints dropped instantly.

> As it turns out, we value time spent waiting differently from time spent walking. And this insight is why you feel like you've run a half marathon to get your bags, and also why you're not unhappy about your wait.
>
> Value shows up in strange places sometimes, and putting yourself in your customers' shoes is a good way to unlock it.

But that was all incidental to the company's well-defined goal: "To play only music you'll love." You need to be open to this additional success, should it happen, but it is not your primary objective.

And because it's not, that means you have to be willing to push back when your customer or partner suggests things that are amorphous or won't add value. We've absolutely had to do that. In software development, it is called *asking for custom development*. A potential customer will say, "It's great that you've got this platform, but we'd like to add this feature and this feature." They start pulling us away from what we do best. It's our job to try to stay true to our core competencies, the things that we do well and can charge a premium for, and the things that will truly make the project a success.

THE KIND OF PEOPLE YOU NEED

In chapter 5, we will discuss the kind of people you need to make this approach work. But let me foreshadow the discussion here. To deliver value as a service, you cannot employ people who are like leaves in the wind—people who just go with the flow. You need people who are assertive—forward-thinking leaders who are focused on outcomes, not processes.

Lots of people can work via the system: "tell them what to do, and they'll do it." These people's efforts are simply not as valuable as they once were to organizations. Computers are taking over this type of work, and they are doing it more accurately, much faster, and at a disruptively lower cost. What you need are people who can figure out what needs to be done and people who can gain agreement from your client before you get under way—and then get the work done.

Creating value in concert with your client or vendor will strike some people as difficult; and, to be blunt, it is. For one thing, creating value requires serious collaboration, which is no simple thing. For another, it will probably require you to change how you go about providing products or services, and change is always difficult.

The natural tendency is to fight change and to try to keep things as they are. It is an understandable strategy, but it is one that is ultimately doomed. Eventually, competition is going to come in, implement the idea of value as a service, and reduce you to a commodity player.

Conversely, if you follow this approach, you stand to make a lot more money. So you have to constantly think about better or different ways to apply what you are good at—your core competencies.

For example, here at Coupa, we're good at creating scalable, integrated technology that's end-user focused. We were in procurement first, and then we said, "What else could we do with this competency of usable, cloud-based technology? What's a similar business process in the existing or ancillary domain? Maybe we could apply the same logic and best practices to that." So we did it for expense management, and we did it for invoice management. Today, we have a comprehensive suite of products that leverage our strength and, at the same time, continue to offer more and more value to customers.

We created all that by doing everything we discussed here. We not only talked to our customers, we walked in their shoes and asked ourselves where we would be trying to save money if we were them. How can we get our arms around more of that transactional spend? Therefore, we've built other tools for them to offer more incremental value.

The course we took is one everyone else will need to follow as well. As companies get more efficient, and competition becomes even more global, either you deliver value as a service or you will be left behind.

TAKEAWAYS

- ▶ The first thing you need to understand, if you are going to offer value as a service, is exactly what value is in each and every case.

- ▶ You don't define that value alone. And your client does not define value alone. You need to do it together—and early on.

- ▶ You and the customer must agree on what success is before you start the work. If you don't, bad things may happen.

WHAT'S AHEAD?

In the next chapter, we turn our attention to the companies that are leveraging the subscription economy, and we will look at some of those companies that are struggling.

CHAPTER 3

VALUE: PAST, PRESENT, AND YOUR FUTURE

Let me begin with the payoff from this chapter: To stay ahead of your competition in the coming years, you will need to consistently offer value as a service. More specifically, you will need to provide quantifiable value to your customers consistently over the life of your relationship with them.

Offering great customer service won't be enough. (Although, providing it is always a good practice.) And customer satisfaction (as we talked about in the last chapter) won't be sufficient to separate you from the pack. You will need to deliver agreed-upon value that can be measured in some specific way. "We save you X dollars every month." Or, "Because you use our product, you are now handling transactions 15 percent faster with 20 percent fewer people." If you can't do this, one of your competitors certainly will, and they will take your customers.

Not only are you going to have to deliver value as a service, but you will have to do it sooner than you think. To understand why, let's take a step back and look at the technology industry, recognizing that the rate of change is fast and only increasing. Given that, what we are advocating will probably become commonplace soon, so you either need to get ready for the future or get left behind. If you doubt us, consider the fate of all the companies in our industry that were around in the 1990s that failed to adapt. As a result, they either went out of business or were acquired for a fraction of what they were once worth.

In case you don't remember what was going on back then, here's the simplest way to put it: Enterprise software was a product-based world and had been for decades. The product was first sold and deployed on mainframes and was later distributed through CDs during the client-server era. But it was always a product. A company would make something physical, put it into a box, and ship that box to a customer.

However, the problem was that a significant portion of big deployments never delivered the kind of value that was anticipated, or worse, they became expensive shelfware. What we had was an abusive kind of relationship, in that all the risk rested with the customer. The customer paid up front, the software company shipped them the product, and then it was up to the customer to make it work. To add insult to injury, customers also had to wait to buy the next iteration to be able to take advantage of any upgrades.

While all that sounds like a great deal for the software providers, it really wasn't. For one thing, they had to deal with functions that were not part of their core competencies—producing the CDs and packaging and distributing them, for example, even if supported through third parties. The business model also made for uneven revenue flow, which meant that the providers scrambled every quarter to make their numbers, resulting in a stressful existence.

The ebbs and flows in new bookings meant that product roadmaps were sacrificed routinely at the altar of revenue. Often, these companies would build whatever it took to bring in a dollar. Yes, the company made (sometimes a lot of) money selling the software. And while it made a bit more by providing maintenance and technical support, the real money was in selling the software. But this business model didn't lead to great sustainable outcomes for anyone.

Enterprise software companies in the 1990s were in the production and transaction business: Produce the CD, sell the CD, and then either go out and find another customer or wait until you had an upgraded version (i.e., another iteration of your product) to sell to your existing customer base.

That's the world that enterprise software companies were living in for a long time, until we got to the current subscription models.

Today, a software company can take their product, install it in a secure, remote virtual environment—whether at their headquarters or on a third-party platform—and have their clients access it through a web browser like Google Chrome or Apple Safari. The way we consume software today is similar to how we consume electricity. There is a remote source that any single customer (or household) can subscribe to in order to receive value, and they pay for what they use. Just like long-distance power transmission technology made it possible for centralized electrical grids to not only exist but become the dominant method of energy transfer, the Internet and broadband technology has made it possible for software to be delivered primarily through the web.

It is clear that software as a service provides a much better value proposition and lower up-front risk to the customer. Before software as a service was an option, if you bought a $3 million product from a software company, you'd own that product, and all the risks that came with it, forever. It was your (the customer's) responsibility to get it to work the way you hoped it would. And whether it did or not, you were still out the $3 million.

With the subscription model, you're still likely to be paying, if you do an apples-to-apples comparison, the same $3 million, but it will be spread out over three years—a million dollars a year for a three-year subscription.

The advantages of the subscription model are obvious:

- ▶ You do not have to pay the entire $3 million all at once.

- ▶ Should the vendor not perform, you can cancel, saving the rest of the subscription price.

- ▶ It's quicker. You get up and running faster. There is less software to configure. You plug directly into the service.

- ▶ You don't have to wait until the next full iteration of the software is available to get upgrades; you can receive them as the vendor completes them and makes them accessible.

- ▶ On a related point, if the vendor is any good, they are incorporating, in real time, key suggestions from anyone who uses the software, so everyone can benefit. (See "One Question *Not* to Ask Your Software-as-a-Service Vendor.")

▶ But the biggest benefit is the shared risk. Because you're paying as you go, you can hold the vendor accountable. If they are not delivering for you, you simply cancel the subscription.

One Question *Not* to Ask Your Software-as-a-Service Vendor

As a software-as-a-service vendor starts to grow, customers and potential customers typically ask what they believe is a relevant question: "Will we get all the attention we need?" It is easy to understand why they ask. Existing customers want to know that they will continue to be special. Potential customers want to know if there will be enough bandwidth for them.

On the surface, the question seems logical. If you're at a busy hotel that only has one concierge, they may not be able to make the restaurant reservations, secure the show tickets, or otherwise give you the personal attention you need to make your visit a smashing success. In that environment, asking "Will we get all the attention we need?" makes sense.

But is this the best question you could be asking your software-as-a-service provider? Not so much. There are better questions to ask.

Here's why: When done right, customer success with software as a service is not so much about individual attention as it is about scalable product development and a delivery that codifies best practices that all customers can benefit from.

If a software vendor is building a custom system for you, yes, individual attention is important. But if the vendor is building a software-as-a-service platform, drawing best practices from hundreds of customers and millions of data points and encoding them into the platform, what

continued on next page

you should be most concerned with is how the company decides what those best practices will be.

This is true for both enterprise and consumer software. Facebook is a good example. You don't join Facebook because of the individual attention they're going to give you. You join and stay with Facebook because they have created a huge community of users all over the world, and because they are figuring out the best ways to do that by continually optimizing functionality.

You've decided you want to enter their world and trust them. This includes trusting that when they make mistakes, they will self-correct. For example, if they throw too many ads into the feed, people using the service will change their behavior, the data will reflect those changes, and Facebook will pull back, reducing the number of ads, or perhaps work to make them even more relevant. They take into account data from millions of users to make these decisions. They learn and adjust.

Of course, Facebook is free for the user, and enterprise software is typically not.

There's a tendency to think that because you're paying a lot of money, you should get more individual attention. To a certain extent, that's true. If you pay enough, you get special attention in terms of a louder voice in feature prioritization and ongoing services support. But that does not make personal attention the most important thing to ask about.

Think of purchasing software as a service for the enterprise as buying a house in a new development. Every house will have a roof and windows and doors and water and electricity. Roads will be built to navigate around the development and connect to nearby streets. Parks and schools will be integrated into the neighborhood.

You may have a choice of a single-family home, townhouse, or condominium, but an engineer or architect or interior designer will have already preselected the best floor plans and finishes, leaving you with the opportunity to configure key critical areas while taking advantage of everything the neighborhood has to offer. What you're really buying is the neighborhood and the community, not just the house.

The questions to ask about your home purchase then become, "Does the builder have a good reputation? Are they using the latest technology and materials? Do I like the architectural style of the houses?" You need to know the vision, the plan for the long term, and who is guiding it.

The same is true when buying into a software-as-a-service platform. Your success is ultimately driven not by individual attention but by whether the software vendor is smart enough to figure out which elements will deliver customer success as both companies—yours and theirs—grow.

The questions for the vendor then become, "What kinds of customers do you have? What is your philosophy for codifying best practices for all customers and, particularly, for the kind of customer that I am? What is your long-term roadmap and strategy for your platform?"

If you ask these kinds of questions, you'll be able to easily avoid the vendors that are custom-code shops and be able to find the ones that will deliver customer success—your success—over the long term.

It's not so much about attention as it is about philosophy.

It's not so much about the house as it is about the neighborhood.

It's about whether you can get the business value you are seeking.

THE VENDOR BENEFITS AS WELL

In the subscription model, the vendor's value drivers are also good.

1. Vendors get the economies of scale that come from running one centralized operation.

2. They can concentrate on their core competencies. (No more production or mailing of disks.)

3. They get to leverage the ideas their users have, and they can incorporate the most impactful enhancements in real time.

4. Perhaps the biggest advantage is a steady revenue stream. In theory, customers will renew for life. No more scrambling from quarter to quarter and being dependent on selling product to generate revenue.

That's a huge deal. Let's go back to the example we used earlier in the chapter. If you get $3 million for selling a piece of software, that's great. But then the next quarter comes, and you're starting at zero in revenue.

If you close that $1 million subscription in the first year, it's true that it's only a third of what you could have gotten selling the software outright. But as you enter year two, you are guaranteed another million. And as long as you did right by the customer, you're going to get another million in year three and perhaps in years four, five, six . . . and beyond.

What you get is a recurring revenue stream, and that results in predictability. Predictability creates stability. It allows you to continuously fine-tune your business instead of scrambling each quarter, trying to make the numbers.

The disadvantage for the vendor is, of course, that they don't get the money up front. It'd be nice to have $3 million right away versus $1 million a year for three years. But other than that, there aren't any real disadvantages. Software as a service is a much more efficient delivery medium for software, and, as we have seen, it is a far better business model as well.

So, if the move to software as a service has so many benefits, why did I hint in the chapter title that to be successful in coming years, you will need to move beyond the way the software-as-a-service business is typically done?

There are two key reasons.

The move to software as a service, while good, still doesn't eliminate all the problems of the past. Vendors are continuing to sell software, although the sale is through a subscription. And on the other side of the table, somebody is buying something; even though it is a subscription, it's still too much like buying a product.

The relationship needs to feel like a partnership well before any negotiation begins. I should not be selling to you, and you should not have fifty lawyers trying to squeeze everything out of me. It ought to consist of both parties creating a common vision of what we want to achieve in terms of business value by applying your insights and our technology. We should enter into the relationship together, with the feeling that if you don't succeed, I don't succeed (see "What to Look for in a Partner").

The second problem is simply Business 101. If everyone moves to this way of doing business, and everyone does it the same way, no one will have a competitive advantage. Everyone will appear the same.

You'll need a way to stand out.

What to Look for in a Partner

We all know how the vendor selection process works. You do a needs analysis, put out a request for proposal (RFP) or a request for quotation (RFQ), compare and contrast the responses, pick one of the respondents, get to work on the project, and celebrate when the work is done.

But when the project is over, it's entirely possible that no meaningful business outcome was attained. Sure, the work was completed, but it could have just been busywork. The company could be no closer to overall success than it was when it started.

Using a software vendor as an example, the ideal customer-vendor relationship should be a partnership focused not on technology deployment but on tangible business outcomes that move your company forward. To achieve that kind of relationship, you need to look beyond line items on an RFP or RFQ and study the approach the vendor takes to the market.

Specifically, you should look for three must-have characteristics:

- **A focus on the bigger picture.** First and foremost, you want a vendor who concentrates on making their customers successful. They should not be focused solely on how much money they can make. They should be focused on getting you to a mutually agreed-upon result. There are plenty of people who create great stopgaps for individual business problems. There aren't too many vendors who are thinking holistically about the customer's business outcome.

- **A minimal-friction approach.** The ideal vendor looks for the most straight-line path to customer results. To me, that means finding places to remove friction and not introducing additional friction into any existing process. What's the difference? Let's discuss two different scenarios. Company *A* comes in and says, "You will have to adopt our tool and roll out our training. You must have people go to this site to do this and follow this procedure to achieve that. Everyone needs to learn to do it our way." Company *B* tries to weave themselves into your existing business processes. They ask, in essence, "How can we effectively map our solution to your challenges?" That's the big difference—the focus is on the result, not the process.

- **An orientation that favors people over process.** Look for a company that is malleable, understands human interactions, and consistently seeks to improve the way it's working. Listen to how they speak. Is it, "Version 6.12 requires you to log into this screen or call this phone number?" If it is, this company is saying they have rigid, bureaucratic processes, and this is how they work, so this is how you will have to work. A people-oriented company questions processes and uses common sense to adjust. One company tries to lay down the law. The other is willing to have a dialogue with you and then will adapt based on your feedback. It's an organism that's evolving in real time. It's the difference between a plant that's growing and a computer monitor that's going to be the same in thirty years, no matter what you do to it.

You have to go beyond the RFP and listen to how vendors talk and understand how they do things. That is how you notice the difference between them.

continued on next page

If you're looking to partner with a vendor who can solve your business problems and not create new ones, look for one that will focus on getting you to a higher level of business success, not one that is simply implementing some technology.

We aren't at that point yet, but it is easy to see how we could get there soon. Let's use a real-world example featuring Salesforce.com, the customer relationship management (CRM) company. The firm has handled the transition to a software-as-a-service world well: Salesforce's toll-free number spells out *no software*, and *Forbes* has named the firm one of America's most innovative companies for four years running.

Suppose you have a subscription with them, and it is just about up. You are likely to renew, because the service is sticky; you already have all your customer data with them, and if they have delivered what they promised, and they haven't jacked the price up too much at renewal time, you are likely to stay. After all, they are a visionary and highly respected company, and on top of that, the difficulty of switching is not worth the hassle.

But perhaps in years to come, transitioning from one CRM service to another will become easy. You'll simply suck your data out of one and drop it into the other. And suppose the other one offers the service at a much lower price with the same, or perhaps better, technology. And let's also assume they're innovating quickly and have more modern technology. That could challenge the likes of a company like Salesforce, because the switching costs have now become low.

In that kind of environment, the price keeps going down to

the point where there is no margin; we are approaching commoditization. Should that happen, what is going to differentiate one subscription software service company from another? My belief is it'll be whether or not companies are able to show real, quantifiable, continuous value from the offering—in other words, value as a service.

If a company is paying $2 million a year in subscription costs, but they are saving $30 million a year—a figure they have been able to quantify—the likelihood of switching becomes much lower. Even if it were easy to switch, the company will seriously consider the risks involved and whether the new vendor will be as good. Yes, they might be able to save $1 million in subscription costs, but the risk of switching for this incremental savings—and the time, energy, and effort it would take—probably won't be worth it to them as long as their current service provider can keep delivering $30 million a year in savings.

That's why I am convinced that the next step in software as a service is value as a service, and companies will soon be stressing that value in their marketing. For example, Salesforce.com, in the next iteration of their advertising and branding, might say things like, "We increased revenues of our typical client by 15 percent within nine months," or, "We improved lead volumes by 12 percent in the first year."

Notice what is going on. In the future, satisfying your customer is simply not going to be sufficient to keep them. They will expect you to do that; it will become the price of entry. You will need to point to something of real economic value in order to keep their business. And that value will be something that you will need to quantify early and often.

As we said in chapter 2, going forward, it will be up to the vendor and customer to determine what value is. And it is possible that the customer could say, "Value is that the software we buy needs to be highly efficient, or it needs to run processes faster." But terms like that are squishy. In this instance, it's hard to know what *highly efficient* or *run faster* exactly mean. That's one reason the value will need to be consistently quantified. You and your customer will agree that the software will run 15 percent faster, or whatever the number is. That will allow you to tell, at a glance, whether the vendor is supplying the agreed-upon value.

Once the value is quantified, you can do the math. "Okay, we agreed our purchase would allow us to handle Process X 15 percent faster. We have twenty people involved in that process, and their fully loaded cost is $100,000 each, or $2 million a year. That means the value provided is $300,000 (15 percent of $2 million), and it also means that the $100,000 purchase we made was a good deal."

If you are the vendor, you can point out that the $300,000 drops to the customer's bottom line, increasing profitability and driving up the client's stock price.

That is the kind of value conversation you can have when you quantify things versus "We are going to do some stuff faster. Trust us."

It isn't surprising that quantifying value is so important. It goes back to the central question, "What is the purpose of the business?" Many people say it is to "create shareholder value" or "create stakeholder value." Regardless of what it is, it's measured off of your balance sheet, income statement, and cash flow. How much money are you creating? How profitable are you? How fast are your revenues growing? It's evaluated in business terms first. In the case of our example, it's how much money did we save?

QUANTIFIABLE VALUE EXISTS EVERYWHERE

The fact that we are looking for quantifiable value from someone we do business with shouldn't be surprising. It is exactly the sort of thing we do in our personal lives. Let me give you an example.

I came into a little bit of money a few years ago, thanks to some luck and a bit of success at a previous job. Someone from one of the major brokerage firms—you'd recognize the name of the company he worked for—called me up and said his firm would like to help me handle that money. I thought, *Great. His firm has the experts. They watch the markets. They have all kinds of ideas that they would share with me, in exchange for taking a small percentage of my money each year as a management fee.* I thought that was fine, because I would benefit from their expertise.

I give the guy the money, and I see the market go up. And it goes down. And then it goes up really high, and I call him and say, "Hey, what do you think? Should we maybe sell a little?"

"No, no," he tells me. "The firm is really bullish long term. Everything is great."

Desperately Needed: A Tighter Alignment Between Software Companies and Implementation Firms

Our focus has been on what you need to do within the walls of your company to be successful in a value-as-a-service world. But you must manage your consultants and vendors as well. Take, for example, the relationship between an enterprise software company you have decided to use and the firm charged with implementing that software.

These partnerships are often given scant consideration, and that

continued on next page

can be a huge problem. You can't say, "We're going to get the best deal on the software, and then we will hire a consultant we know and marry them." That is not optimal.

Most software companies are good at technology. Implementation services firms are typically good at configuration and consulting. At first glance, these seem to be distinct competencies that can easily be snapped together. But as with most of life, the devil is in the details. And if the partnership is not a good fit, things can quickly be reduced to finger pointing.

The consultant says, "Well, we did a gap analysis, and we found where the process-to-technology gaps are, and for that, we're charging you money." They think their value added is to analyze your business and tell you to build or buy something.

The technology provider says, "Hey, our technology can do whatever you want. It's the implementation guys who are misunderstanding it. They have no idea what they're doing besides milking you for services dollars."

While they bicker, the customer loses out.

The client needs to look hard at the partnership, with an eye toward finding those firms that know how to work together to get the customer to a place of success. And that is the key. It is not about automating what you have done in the past. It is about helping the company redesign the way it does work, so it can succeed in the future.

Clients need to state this clearly, and then they need to make sure both the enterprise software provider and the implementation firm are truly focused on their success. To make sure they are, the client needs to ask serious questions of both firms:

- Have they worked together before?

- Is the implementation partner certified by the software company?

- Do they adhere to similar customer success–oriented values?

- How do they measure joint success for a customer?

- Are they willing to commit to working together as a seamless team to make the customer successful?

It should be clear that both firms understand the transformative nature of what you, the client, are trying to achieve, and that it will be a marriage between process change and technology adoption.

For that to happen, their incentives must be aligned. If one partner is trying to bill as many hours as they can, and the other partner is trying to charge as much as possible for the software, they simply aren't aligned around your success.

Then one day, when the market's really low, I call the guy asking if we should sell, and he says, "No, no. It's just a blip. Keep focused on the long term. Hold steady."

After a couple of years interacting with this guy, I realized that he was just satisfying me. He was helping manage my emotions through the ups and downs of the market. But that was his only real value added, quite frankly, because he put my money into five mutual funds and kept them there for the whole two years I was with him. The funds underperformed the market as a whole, and when you factored in the management fee they were charging me, I was really behind.

He made me feel better when I called, and he was a great guy.

But at the end of the day, you know what I cared about? I wanted him to make me more money than the market. And I didn't care if he invited me to wine and cheese parties where members of his firm spoke, or if he was nice to me. If I need friends, I'll make friends somewhere else. So I pulled my money out.

You might be experiencing the same sort of thing in your business dealings. I know we are in our industry. We're delivering software via a subscription instead of selling a product, but our customers want more than that. They want us to be focused on their success. As the pressures of global hypercompetition kick in, switching costs get lower, and commoditization pressures increase, it's going to come down to what it is that you're actually doing—whether or not you are making the customer successful—that's going to make the difference.

It will take a mind shift to make this work. We are going to have to start looking at customers not as customers, but clients. Why? Because a customer is someone who buys something, almost in a one-off, transactional way. It's like McDonald's. "Oh, we have this many customers that buy our burgers, fries, or whatever." A client relationship goes beyond that.

But what we have been discussing is the opposite of one-time transactions. We have been talking about how to make a corporate marriage work, not about optimizing your next round of speed dating. We have been discussing a long-term, ongoing, client-type relationship that must be focused on quantifiable value creation. Software as a service is the first step in the shift to longer-term relationships. But it is only the first step. The second is to provide quantifiable value that keeps the relationship going. We're moving from transactional, one-time relationships to ongoing ones.

PEOPLE

Even though we are going to talk about this in depth in chapter 5, let me flag something here: To make all this work, companies will need to create a culture that has a customer success—not satisfaction—orientation.

If you are shipping a product, the company is engineering focused. It's products oriented. It's focused on near term: What's the next product we sell? When does it launch?

Think about any products company. Let's take clothing, for example. You're the lead designer for a high-fashion clothing company. You decide what's in fashion. This season, we will offer these kinds of blouses, these kinds of accessories, or whatever it may be. And for whatever reason, let's say nobody likes your clothes.

You know what? The next season, you're going to try again. And the next season, you may have different colors. You may have different styles. You may have different approaches. That's all great. You get another chance. If you annoy the customer, it's not that big a deal. You will be able to offer them something else soon.

> *One way to significantly increase the likelihood of your company's success is to choose individuals and companies to work with that commit to staying aligned and focused on the only thing that matters in the end: measurable customer value.*

But in a subscription business, your orientation has to be around maintaining the customer—keeping the customer forever. That's why you're spending so much money up front to get that million-dollar-a-year subscription versus the $3 million you could receive selling the software. Anyone in a subscription-service-economy business has to be focused on long-term customer success. There is no other way.

When you get the $3 million up front, you don't have to worry, in theory, for three years. When you get $1 million, you've got to worry. Even if you have a contract that says they owe you for two more years, the reality is that the customer could still walk away if they believe you have not performed. Yes, you could sue them, but you don't want to be in a position of suing your customers. The reality is that they can walk, and if they walk, you don't have the money. Cash, at the end of the day, is the fuel for your company.

So you have to make the arrangement work. That's the point. In subscription services, you're playing the long game versus the short game. You need to invest accordingly, and a huge part of that investment is with your people. You either have to retrain your employees so that they acquire this different mind-set, or you have to hire a different type of person. The orientation has to shift. It needs to be less, "We have to ship this on time" or, "We have to deliver this or that," and it needs to be more, "What do we have to do to make our customer successful?"

You need to get your people to a place where they shift their mind-set from near-term customer satisfaction to longer-term customer success. Again, we will talk about how you do that in chapter 5.

A ONCE-IN-A-LIFETIME LAND GRAB

From a vendor's perspective, the move to software as a service and then to value as a service represents a once-in-a-lifetime opportunity.

It's no different than what happened in the record industry. Music was a product industry for so long. First you bought wax cylinders and 78s. Then, we moved on to 45s and LPs, then eight-tracks, then cassettes, and then CDs. After that came pay-as-you-go music. You are able to buy any song you want for ninety-nine cents through services like iTunes.

> **You need to create a customer-success-oriented company, because you are trying to keep your customer forever.**

Today, you have the subscription model via Pandora, Spotify, Rdio, Rhapsody, and the like. You get on Pandora, for instance, and that's your new radio. That's now the delivery medium for your music, and it is a subscription. As long as it's delivering value for you and you're successful with it, you're not going anywhere. Why would you switch? And if you don't, Pandora owns you for as long as they provide value as a service, and increasingly, they can prove that value with metrics: how quickly they access a song you like, how accurate they are in identifying the music you like, and so on.

So it's like a land grab, or really like a gold rush, to go from these nonsticky-products businesses to a once-in-a-lifetime subscription-services business.

Enterprise software is evolving in a similar way. Let's go back to Salesforce.com to show how they might hold onto their customers forever. If you're storing all of your customer data, your opportunities, your contacts, your leads, and your contact information for all your customers in Salesforce, which is a subscription business, and you're paying X dollars per month to access that information and collaborate with your colleagues about what would make your customers successful, why in the world would you ever leave? It's unlikely you would.

As long as Salesforce keeps up, generally, with innovation, utilizing the best and latest technology, and they help make you successful in measurable ways that show you how you benefit, your data will probably stay there.

Just compare Salesforce to Siebel. Siebel was a products business. Salesforce, with its subscription model, disrupted Siebel's model, and they are now worth much more than Siebel ever was.

Barnesandnoble.com versus Amazon is another example. Remember when the e-commerce battle used to be called *brick and mortar versus the web*? Few thought Amazon had a chance. People asked why Barnes & Noble couldn't just put up a website and put Amazon out of business.

But what those people didn't understand was that Amazon was offering value as a service. The value was remarkable convenience, which could be measured by things like how quickly you could locate what you were looking for, how quickly you could put it in your electronic shopping cart and check out, and how quickly you could hold your purchase in your hands. Amazon did this first for books, then for a wide variety of products that continues to grow every day (adding even more value for customers). They have innovated in big ways on the logistics front, with free two-day shipping with Amazon Prime, and they are now experimenting with same-day shipping via drones. They have become the retail distribution arm, and they own every part of the customer experience. With Amazon, the customer relationship became so sticky so quickly that it turned out to be almost impenetrable.

WHAT CAN WE LEARN FROM ALL THIS?

The orientation toward the customer occurs in two steps. The first step is giving customers what they are asking for. In the case of enterprise software, for example, it was an alternative to buying a product. (They wanted software as a service, and technology innovations made that possible.)

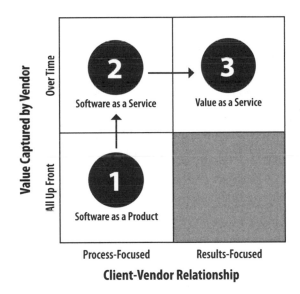

The second step is to ask how a product can be delivered in the most efficient and scalable way possible—a way that provides value as a service that can be quantified and understood by all parties.

TAKEAWAYS

- ▶ Software as a service is only a stopping point on the industry's evolutionary road. It is certainly better for the customer and the providers. But it is not the end destination.

- ▶ We are going to have to move beyond providing software as a service to providing value as a service, where you can quantify exactly what you are providing to your customers.

- ▶ The way to make this happen is to create a true partnership—with value creation at its center—between client and supplier. Then, the vendor must deliver that value or face the risk of being replaced by someone else who will.

WHAT'S AHEAD?

Moving from one way of doing business to another is always difficult. Next, we discuss those companies that were able to make the transition to providing value as a service and those that weren't, so we can learn what works and what doesn't.

CHAPTER 4

SANDWICHES, STATES, AND SKYSCRAPERS: CASE STUDIES IN VALUE CREATION

I n my office, I have two bookcases that hold a couple hundred business books. I bought and read some of those books because I had to and some I read because I wanted to, but in both categories, most of the content was forgettable. Why? There are the typical reasons: They are full of indigestible jargon; a bunch of buzzwords packaged as business breakthroughs; and a collection of "silver bullets" guaranteed to solve the problems of any company, of any size, anywhere—and (of course) they did not.

But if there is a commonality among all the books that are now collecting dust on my shelves, it is this: They all make whatever change they were advocating sound too easy. Much like the diet or weight-loss infomercials I frequently see on television, the authors of these books make you believe that your success in implementing change is a foregone conclusion—"all" you have to do is this or that. All you have to do is get your people to think completely differently or radically alter the way you deal with suppliers or "merely" totally redo your sourcing approach or how you handle partnerships.

The authors dismiss in a sentence or two—if they address the topic at all—how difficult it is to alter a business practice or simply to get folks to change their patterns.

As you and I know, change in the real world isn't easy. And that brings us to what this chapter is all about.

> **Value as a service** *means that you strive to create value for your clients in every interaction, every day, every year for the duration of your relationship. Whether you will be able to do so hinges on your ability to fully institutionalize the changes needed to bring your organization to a higher standard of excellence.*

I have been advocating having your company move to a value-as-a-service business model. And the fact that I just used the phrase *move to* underscores that we are talking about change. And any change, even positive change, is difficult and frequently messy.

That can be the case involving the implementation of value as a service, even though the idea is pretty basic.

As all industries become hypercompetitive, companies will need a way to differentiate themselves. I believe the best way to articulate that differentiation will be by providing demonstrable quantifiable value in every single transaction and customer interaction, and that is where value as a service comes in. It is a method of execution that appears to be the logical next step in business evolution.

At the highest level, that is the reason you want to employ value as a service—to stay ahead of the competition. Right below that, there are two other reasons you will want to follow this approach:

1. To increase your top line (i.e., to increase revenues)

2. To improve your bottom line (by cutting costs)

In either case, you must quantify whatever changes you make. There is no room for vagueness. For example, when we work with a client, they might say that they want to increase efficiency. That sounds good, but how do you do it? Well, you can measure the gap between where they are now and where they want to be, and put a number on it. The kind of increased efficiency they are talking about might be processing invoices in three days instead of sixty or streamlining processes so they can cut staff by 10 percent. No matter what it is, there are a million ways to measure the improvements they want to make.

But differing measures—faster processing times versus lower personnel count—can be difficult to compare head-to-head. That's why you want to reduce those measures to the least common dominator, so that you can easily do a comparison. And one key metric everyone understands is dollar savings.

Journey to Success

Customer View	Unsatisfied	Satisfied	Successful
Vendor Approach	Products company	Software as a service company	Business results company

That, in a nutshell, is what we have been talking about so far: Making sure your business is aligned—both inside and out—to achieve real, measurable customer success. Having a specific dollar figure as a goal helps a lot in gaining that alignment and in driving a certain efficiency in the change you are wanting to implement.

But in many cases, achieving that new alignment means changing the way business gets done. So we are back to the problem of how to make that change.

Because, as I said, change does not always occur smoothly, I want to give you case studies—both positive and negative. We can learn from each.

Let's start with the one that didn't go the way we hoped it would.

At Coupa, we were thrilled to get a chance to work with Subway, the sandwich shop chain that has more than 44,000 restaurants in 111 countries.

Subway has a typical franchise ownership structure where thousands of its stores are owned and operated by franchisees worldwide. Not surprisingly, that diffuse ownership can lead to inefficiencies.

To try to gain some economies of scale, the franchisees created an independent purchasing cooperative (IPC), which procures the ingredients as well as the equipment, supplies, and services used in the restaurants.

We were brought in to try to help improve operations by doing such things as simplifying their ordering system. For example, in the United States alone, the IPC was ordering from over fifteen different food vendors, and they didn't have a lot of visibility into which franchisee was ordering from whom (and sometimes the franchisees would order food directly from a supplier, bypassing the IPC completely).

Quality wasn't a problem, although from time to time, a franchisee would order from someplace like Costco, but there were clearly inefficiencies in the way things were being done. Not only were there places the IPC and their members could save money, but by consolidating buying, they could also smooth out the ordering, making sure they didn't have too much of one item—which could lead to waste, if it didn't sell—and not enough of another. (When meatball subs are one of your big sellers, you never want to run out of meatballs.)

This was a target-rich environment. Everyone agreed there was a lot of opportunity. And that, ironically, was the problem. When you have countless things you can work on, people go off in all kinds of different directions, because there are so many attractive choices. Unless you have specific success goals or metrics—such as we want to reduce spoilage by $500 per month—it is nearly impossible to focus.

And we could never get that focus.

A winning formula:

Shared risk between vendor and customer + complete alignment on goals = Success-oriented approach.

Without that alignment, success is unlikely to happen.

While Subway, obviously, had influence over the IPC, it was independent. And its board of directors was composed of some of the largest franchisees—men and women worth tens of millions of dollars who owned dozens of Subway stores, people who were used to having their own way.

Some of them understood the need to focus on what would constitute successful business metrics. (For example, "We need to simplify the ordering so that it's faster and eliminates mistakes.") Some didn't. And the ones who didn't wanted to focus on what their specific stores needed or how the system itself would work. (For example, there was an endless debate about the exact wording that would take you to the next page on the ordering screen. Honest.)

The IPC had us meet with the franchisees—we attended three separate annual franchisee conventions—and that only made things worse. Every conversation we had, we got pulled in a new direction. Imagine getting passes to Disneyworld, getting there, and not going on any rides all day because you couldn't choose between them. That's how we felt. Just about everyone had different thoughts about what could be done to improve their business. We could try to satisfy all of them, but as we talked about earlier, that isn't an approach you want to take. You don't want to satisfy customers, you want to make them successful, and collectively, the Subway franchisees could never get their hands around what would make them successful. There never was clarity about what the project was about. Should we make it easier to order from suppliers by tying the franchisees directly into the suppliers' systems? Should we ensure that the franchisees never ran out of stock? Should we simplify the steps it took to place an order, or . . .

And equally important was, what were we not going to do?

On top of all this, the IPC couldn't agree on how to measure value from the project in any meaningful way. It wasn't measured in quantifiable terms, such as, "We're going to decrease the amount of time that it takes a manager running a Subway franchise to reorder paper products by 20 percent, which will give them the opportunity to spend that time on customer service."

When it came to making improvements, no one knew where they wanted to go. They just wanted to go live, but what did that mean? Despite the myriad of challenges we overcame (and some, we, as Coupa, never overcame) in terms of technology scale, integration, and change management, we did go live at a few thousand stores. But we did not know if we were being successful, since we didn't know what success meant in this case. And if you don't know where you are going, you'll never get there, and that was our experience with Subway.

We never got anything of real significance done in terms of business value creation, and eventually we jointly agreed with Subway to put the project on hold indefinitely until we figured out whether or not there was something there that would produce real value for the company.

AN INSPIRING FIASCO

Here's another typical situation, and it happened in our own field: spend optimization.

At Coupa, we weren't involved in the following in any way, but it is worth understanding because the story is so representative of a massive undertaking that implodes on itself if it is not handled carefully, and it shows what kind of challenges you can be up against when you try to create something new.

The situation began with such high hopes. The state of Florida was a market leader and an early adopter in government e-procurement technology. They invested in a big way to create their online purchasing program.

Unfortunately, the deployment took longer than everyone would have liked, and in the end, the system had fewer features than everyone had hoped for, but finally, MyFloridaMarketPlace (MFMP) launched.

The software was up and running, but it didn't work as well as expected. Adoption was low, and the tens of millions of dollars of anticipated savings never happened.

The state legislature was not happy.

The problem was that the system Florida had created was neither simple nor intuitive to use. It required too much training. And people were not required—or even encouraged—to use it. Because the complicated new system was opt-in only, many people simply opted not to use it. Going around the system was easy, because the old, bureaucratic workflow was left in place.

In the end, only half of the eligible state agencies ended up using the MFMP program, and those that did used it sporadically.

Worse, the state didn't even end up with a completely streamlined procure-to-pay (P2P) process. Even though items were being procured electronically, paper invoices in many cases were still coming in to the various agencies, where they had to be checked and verified, then sent out to various finance departments, where they were checked and verified again. The approval process remained as overly complicated as ever, despite the new MFMP.

The bottom line? The MFMP largely failed to meet the goals of the state of Florida with half-hearted adoption by the few agencies that did use it.

This sort of scenario happens all the time in the private sector as well. The existing paper-based system might be old and clunky, but it's familiar enough to stay with, especially if the alternative (even if it works better) is complicated.

It doesn't matter how good your software is if people won't use it.

In retrospect, thinking about the lack of adoption of the MFMP system, no one took into account the employees who had to use the system every day. But the problems were worse than that. "[The MFMP system was] hampered by poor project governance, lack of standard procurement processes . . . uneven executive sponsorship, and continued dependence on older shadow systems and work-arounds," reported the *Tampa Bay Times*.

The state wasted tens of millions in opportunity costs—and even more money than that to clean up the mess the ineffective system created. Perhaps even worse, it missed out on efficiencies in being able to understand more about its spend (i.e., who was buying what), and it also missed out on aggregating its spend. If it had that information, it would have had the ability to negotiate better rates or consolidate what they were buying (getting a discount in the process). They could have saved a lot of money!

So what happened as a result of this failure? What did Florida do in response to this less-than-successful effort? Very little. The system is still in place! A little over ten years later, they went and did it all over again. They reintroduced the same software, this time in new-and-improved form. But the results were the same—minority adoption, with redundant systems still functioning.

And the complicated invoice process . . . Well, that stayed the same, too.

The awful results were also the same.

This story is a true debacle, yet what went wrong in Florida is absolutely common. It's so totally endemic to organizational bureau-cracies that we were inspired to ask, *Why does it have to be this way?*

The answer is, of course, it doesn't.

As you read the story about the MFMP, you realize there was never any real clarity between the state of Florida and its technology ven-dors on what they were trying to achieve together. It was a conceptual design at best. It may have sounded like this: "Oh, let's have a market-place. We have all the supplies coming in and all these things we are buying, and we could streamline the process." But that is not a quan-tifiable goal. Were they trying to save money? If yes, how much? Were they trying to increase competition? If yes, by how much? Were they creating the marketplace to increase access to a unified buying pool? If that were the case, how many municipalities needed to be involved in the first three months or in the first year to justify the expenditure? (We will talk about this in detail later in the chapter.)

There were no success criteria defined.

As I said in chapter 2, when we were discussing all the technical problems with the Affordable Care Act rollout, this lack of clarity happens all the time—in both the public and private sectors. If there isn't complete clarity around what exactly we want to do, then how can we possibly measure if we are going to get there? We can't. And as the Florida and Affordable Care Act website examples show, the result will be suboptimal every time.

What would we have done if someone from the state of Florida had called us, after it was clear they had a problem with the MFMP, and said, "Can you help save us?"

Well, the first thing we'd do is ask, "How do you define *saving us?* Clearly, you have a problem, but what is it that you're trying to achieve?"

This, by the way, is the sort of question we ask all the time. We call it *forward posturing*. We say something like this: "Let's assume we start working together, and consultants get involved, and software gets evaluated. Lots of plane tickets are bought so we can see one another, and lots of meetings are held. Three years pass, and everyone has worked really hard. How will we know whether our joint efforts—your efforts, my efforts, your team's efforts, my team's efforts—have produced something that generated something that has measurable outcome, that has real value?"

In other words, what does *mission accomplished* look like? Is it that all departments within the state of Florida have access to the marketplace and have decreased their spending by 15 percent? Is it that orders are being placed 20 percent faster and with 10 percent fewer people? What are the specific goals?

And once we know what they are, I'd ask, "Are you willing to make the trade-off decisions to get there? Are you willing not to send me a three-hundred-page request for proposal (RFP) document for all of the things you would like to have, and instead include only things you need to achieve your goals? Are you willing to tie people's bonuses to achieving specific objectives? In other words, are you truly committed to making this program a success?"

Yes, I know what the pushback is going to be. In the case of government, they are going to tell me politics are involved, that we need to include certain things to satisfy certain constituencies. But that is no different than what happens in the private sector. In any project anywhere, you're going to have a lot of constituents who want different things. And obviously, all those different wants need to be considered. But, as we have talked about, it is impossible to satisfy everyone. Trying to do that only guarantees that you will produce a watered-down product or service—one that is not going to be particularly effective.

There needs to be a unified, guiding set of principles and, most importantly, a clear set of measurable success criteria for the deployment. And that means the people in charge need to be able to separate the *nice to haves* and focus on *must haves* first. In the case of the state of Florida, for example, if the ultimate goal is to have a balanced budget, then everyone involved needs to agree on which three things need to get done to make it happen.

But in the case of Florida's rollout of MFMP, that kind of clarity never occurred.

ON THE BRIGHT SIDE

In contrast, consider the work we did for AECOM. Like the Florida rollout, it was a complex project, but unlike the State of Florida, AECOM had strong clarity about what they were trying to achieve.

AECOM is a Fortune 500 company with more than $19 billion in annual revenue. The massive construction firm operates all over the world, but it did not have one unified way of accounting for costs. (That was not surprising. Just about every project had its own cost structure, and costs associated with each project were charged to that project.)

At the highest levels, the company was clear that it wanted to change and was equally clear on what its goals were. It wanted to go from having zero spending under management to 80 percent spending under management. And that goal was set at the top of the organization. Unless you get the C-level to make the call about what they want to accomplish, it is hard to get people aligned. Everyone will have their own agendas, as we saw with Subway.

Understanding a change like the one that AECOM wanted would not happen overnight, so management set an interim goal of saving $10 million during the first phase of the project. This process is, obviously, in stark contrast to what Subway and the state of Florida did.

Another key difference? Neither Subway nor Florida had a lot of experience rolling out a new software program organization-wide. That wouldn't have been a problem if they had focused on specific goals. But since they didn't, it just compounded the problems. AECOM had lots of experience in software rollouts, and because they were focused on the end goal, it was easier for them to stay on track when the inevitable problems arose.

And, of course, they did.

AECOM had all their financials in Oracle, which is a big, monolithic application. AECOM (through Oracle) was tracking something like sixty thousand individual projects, and the challenge was to get a handle on the overall spending (i.e., what they were paying for concrete, labor, services, and everything else they used in each project). That was a big task, and it was compounded by the fact that they were calling certain costs one thing and our software was designed to record it as something else. So every time an expenditure happened, we'd have to go back and reconcile the two systems. We'd have to push back into their system and pull back into ours for a lot of disparate data. This meant that there were transactional integration points across thousands of projects, requiring that Coupa and Oracle interact with each other literally thousands of times per day in order to stay in sync. But because we knew what we were trying to accomplish, it made it easier to solve those challenges. Ultimately, the integrated teams, composed of employees of both AECOM and Coupa, delivered against the set of success criteria, resulting in massive value creation for everyone.

QUANTITATIVE CONSIDERATIONS

How can you make sure you are focused on creating success for your clients? It begins with a major mind shift. You move from a process orientation (these are the things we do, day-to-day procedures) to a goal orientation (i.e., here's what we need to accomplish specifically in order to be successful). You change from concentrating on activities to the outcomes we need to accomplish (and how are we going to do it?).

> *Success equals quantifiable value.*

As you make this shift, you want to keep the following things—both positive and negative—in mind. Let's start with the negative.

1. You never want to port your old ways of doing things onto a new process or technology. In other words, you can't assume that because you employ a new technology, the same process will somehow get better. That's one of the biggest mistakes you can make. If the process wasn't working as well as it should to begin with, the new technology is probably not going to solve whatever problems you were having.

2. Similarly, you should never constrain yourself with your previous way of reasoning. A *this-is-the-way-things-have-always-been-done-around-here* kind of thinking should be eliminated. Part of the reason you're investing in new initiatives is that you want best practices to enter your organization. Let them.

3. I know I have said this already, but I can't stress it enough. You should not kick off a new initiative or program, or introduce a new process or piece of software, unless you're 100 percent certain of what your objectives are, and you have gotten broad alignment with most of the key constituents around the objectives. It's not just that you know what you're trying to accomplish—although that is vital—it is that everyone around you does too, and you have gotten buy-in from all the people who you need to make it happen.

4. Never trust consultants to do the heavy lifting for you. You should never ask, or expect, them to write those goals for you. You could trust them to give you advice, but ultimately, you ought to hold yourself accountable for determining what those goals should be.

On the positive side, you want to set the following sorts of quantifiable success metrics. (The list is meant to be illustrative, not exhaustive.)

▶ Increase the number of people who are using the new program or process by 20 percent.

- ▶ Increase cost savings. We want to save this much in dollars or cut the current spending by 15 percent, for instance.

- ▶ Gain visibility. Today we have 20 percent visibility into the places where we're spending money. We want to improve that by 300 percent. So three months from now we want to have 60 percent visibility.

- ▶ Improve our on-time deliveries by 25 percent, or cut the time it takes to process a purchase order in half.

- ▶ Make sure we can get early payment discounts (a reduction of 2 percent if you pay within ten days would be an example of what we are talking about here) 100 percent of the time.

- ▶ Improve our compliance with company policies from 75 percent to 95 percent. That would include making sure people aren't buying things they are not supposed to.

- ▶ Track against best practice benchmarks. Today we are at 80 percent of best in class. By this time next year, we will be at 90 percent.

What would be your next step? Well, once you have complete clarity on the goal, you could list all of the obstacles that would prevent you from successfully completing that goal. And underneath every obstacle, you could delineate methods for overcoming them. So on top, you might have the goal. The level below could contain three obstacles. And then below these obstacles, you might have six different ways of overcoming each.

Then you would determine the path of least resistance to overcoming each challenge and getting to the outcomes you want.

DO THE MATH

You could set a measurable objective, like saying your goal is to save the company $12 million within the next year (or whatever period of time you choose). But is that a good thing?

It sounds like a silly question, doesn't it?

But it isn't really. If it costs you $15 million to save $12 million, you are falling behind. That's why you need to know how much that change management program—or whatever initiative we are talking about—designed to save the $12 million is going to cost you. More specifically, in the case of a purchase of a software subscription, for example, you need to calculate with a certain degree of accuracy how much it will cost to buy the software, implement the software, maintain the software, and get the people around the organization that need to be involved to interface with the software (i.e., use the software). You must go through the change management that's required to implement anything new—including a new cost-saving initiative—and figure out every cost so you have a sound business case that you can track against on both the improvement side (i.e., the value or saving side) and on the cost side to hold yourself accountable.

As many know, every time you do something new—especially if it involves an IT project—you have to make a business case. You have to create a return on investment (ROI) model. You have to build a total cost of ownership (TCO) model. And the truth is, most would agree, that those analyses get done, but they would also agree that those analyses end up getting tossed out the window about five seconds after the purchase decision gets made, and are never revisited. I'm serious. Of course, I am speaking in broad strokes, but it's largely true. You and I know it happens all time.

But that shouldn't be the case. Not only do you need to do the math when you want to justify a major new investment, you need to track it as well. You need to track whether or not your financial objectives are being achieved over time. You need to determine what your true ROI and TCO are.

The good news is, leaders of your business have asked executives and others to justify the investment before it is made. That is absolutely the right thing to do. But probably one of the things they're not doing right is they're not holding people accountable for ensuring that they monitor the investment for value over the long term.

My guess is that will change and probably fairly soon. Operational efficiencies and competitive dynamics will force people to prove that they are getting ongoing value as a service from their providers. And the providers that are best suited to justify that will stand the test of time and thrive. There needs to be ongoing savings, especially when you provide a subscription service. It can't be a one-time thing.

Yes, We Practice What We Preach

This book is not intended to be a commercial, nor are we particularly comfortable bragging about ourselves.

That said, people ask us all the time if here at Coupa we practice what we preach. Do we provide value as a service? The short answer is we try to every day. As for a longer answer, we figured the easiest— and most objective—way to answer the question was to let a handful of our clients respond for us.

We asked those clients to highlight a key benefit or two they received from working with us and then to quantify the savings or

---

economic gains they received over a twelve-month period. So the numbers you are about to read come from them, not us.

Here's what they said. (You can watch and hear most of them and more if you go to http://www.coupa.com/results/.)

- Cliff Gott, director of nonmerchandise purchasing, Fresh Market (the publicly held two-hundred-store chain that has supermarkets in more than half the country): "We open on average twenty stores per year. Coupa has allowed us to support our stores with less people in the back office than we had three years ago." Among the advantages of working with Coupa were the following: Fresh Market reduced the time to process a purchase order from fifteen minutes to five. That worked out to be a savings of $7 per PO. Since the company handled 51,988 POs in the last year, that alone saved the company $363,916. The total twelve-month savings were $1,809,320.

- Rone Luczynski, managing director of supply chain management, Service Corporation International, the $2 billon-plus-in-revenues funeral services firm. Among the advantages we provided were the following: We reduced supplier overpayments by $1.3 million and allowed the company to take $500,000 in early payment discounts. The total twelve-month savings were $6,660,603.

- Mike Van Gerven, NEC (the $8 billion-in-sales global electronics firm) head of procurement for Europe, Middle East, and Africa. Among the advantages was a 50 percent reduction in purchase order approval time. The total twelve-month savings were $2,000,814.

continued on next page

- Curt Metzger, director of finance, Concentrix Corp (whose 70,000 people operate in twenty-five countries). Among the advantages we provided were a $16 million savings compared with the supplier they had been using. We cut the cost of processing 56,000 invoices, 32,000 POs, and 30,000 expense reports by $840,000. The total twelve-month savings were $30,440,685.

- David NewVine, vice president of $25 billion-in-assets First-Merit Bank, which serves the Midwest. Among the advantages were a 30 percent reduction in hand-keyed invoices, and we decreased the cost of issuing purchase orders by 50 percent. The total twelve-month savings were $3,110,590.

- Jeff Gray, procure to pay manager, $42 billion-in-assets Silicon Valley Bank. Among the advantages we provided were being able to build auditor compliance questions into purchase acquisition requisitions, saving $10 per invoice processed, and taking advantage of early payment discounts. The total twelve-month savings were $15,839,387.

- Hyrum Kirton, vice president procurement, Avalon Health Care, which operates in Utah, Arizona, California, Washington, and Hawaii. Among the advantages we provided were reducing the number of people processing invoices from sixty to twelve and getting invoices approved in less than eight hours when it used to take three days. The total twelve-month savings were $5,522,468.

THE CASE FOR CHANGE

In the abstract, it is difficult to make a case against what we have talked about here. Everyone wants to provide value to their customers.

But business does not happen in the abstract. And as we said at the outset of the chapter, change is difficult. Inertia and entrenched ways of doing business can be compelling forces of resistance. You know the pushback: "We have systems in place, people know what to do now, and it has taken us years to get to the point where we are now. We don't want to change."

I understand. But if you don't adopt this mind-set, you are likely to be less operationally efficient than your competition. You are going to have slack in your business, and that slack over time, in a hypercompetitive business environment, is going to slow down your revenue growth and cause you to lose market share or become less profitable. Ultimately, you are going to be worth less to your shareholders and stockholders if you don't change. And this is true for every industry.

The funny thing about this is that if you don't do it, the fact that you will start falling behind won't be immediately obvious. The harmful effects of your operational inefficiencies won't be easily observed until it's too late. It will be as if you are a boat with a tiny crack and the water is coming in a drip at a time. It may take some time, but the boat will eventually sink. That's why having the mind-set of providing value as a service earlier on will put you in a better position to stay afloat and remain competitive. You'll be more nimble, efficient, and (ultimately) successful.

TAKEAWAYS

- ▶ If you don't know where you are going, you will never get there. Before you begin, there needs to be clear agreement on the specific goals for the project.

- ▶ There can be lots of debate up front about what the goals should be. But once they are set, everyone needs to agree to them and then try their best to make them a reality.

- ▶ Having the goals in mind will make it easier to solve the inevitable problems that crop up. Everyone will be able to work toward a common solution with the end goal in mind.

WHAT'S AHEAD?

How do you create a corporate culture that is relentlessly focused on value creation?

CHAPTER 5

VALUES CREATE VALUE: WHY YOUR CULTURE MATTERS

S o how do you do it?

How do you create a company that is devoted to creating value, one that is dedicated to making its customers successful?

The typical (and easy) answer is to say, "It starts at the top." And for some old-line companies, that may be right.

This top-down approach can be accomplished when you work in a highly regimented industry that is resistant to change: where innovation is unnecessary, entrepreneurial behavior takes a backseat to process-driven thinking, and operational discipline is often sufficient for success.

For example, maybe you're part of a centuries-old manufacturing company, and all you need is a foreman or a plant manager telling employees what to do, or you need to figure out how to get the assembly line to go faster.

However, in an information-driven economy, especially if you work for a knowledge company, as most companies are today, I don't think the top-down approach is the way to go, for at least three reasons—and two of them have to do with the way the organizational chart is typically constructed and construed.

If you think about the typical organizational chart, with the CEO at the top and the least senior people at the bottom, the assumption is that the people at the top have all the answers.

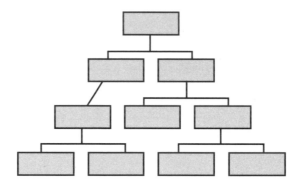

As a CEO, I can tell you we don't. We have experience and a certain set of skills and expertise. But a lock on all knowledge? No. And we should not be seen that way. Instead of being viewed as people who tell the organization what to do at all times, our role should be to support the company and our employees as they take care of our customers and help them be successful. (I'll talk more about that in a minute.)

The second problem with the traditional org chart is all the linkages and interconnected lines you see. The implicit—and real—message they send is that if you are not at the top of the chart, you need to get approvals for just about everything you do from all those above you. How frustrating is that?

And that brings us to the third point.

Not only do you have to get approvals, the org chart—with all its reporting lines—makes clear that the people above you are going to tell you what to do. No one wants to spend the entire day at work being bossed around. People—especially millennials—want to have a way to express themselves at work. They don't want to be ordered about.

It is clear from all this that the traditional org chart doesn't work well today. It is inhibiting to a knowledge-worker environment where creative- and qualitative-type work is being asked for.

Just as blindly mapping your old ways onto a new process or technology makes little sense (as we discussed in chapter 4), we realized that replicating a culture that was optimized for the Industrial Revolution did not make sense for us either. So we started to think about alternative structures.

We thought about having a free-flowing culture, where work-groups are created around their own projects. They would innovate, try different things, and then take them to market. It's an intriguing structure, especially for research and development (R&D) groups that are charged with coming up with game-changing innovations. Nine out of ten fail, but one out of ten can change the world, as Google has shown.

But that way of organizing didn't make sense for our business. We couldn't figure out how we would be able to provide value as a service on a consistent basis company-wide with that approach.

So we literally decided to flip the org chart on its head and created an upside-down org chart. What this new structure says is that my job as a senior leader is not to tell my employees what to do and then have them go do it, but rather to create an environment and a support structure for them to stretch themselves and leverage their strengths and their aspirations to drive the company forward.

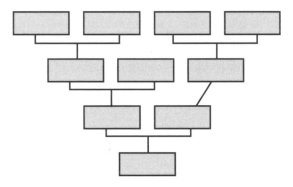

Inverting the org chart was the right thing to do. It made sense to have as many people as possible doing all that they could to help our customers succeed. I really do believe the adage that all of us are smarter than any one of us.

Okay, so far so good.

But remember, we are trying to create a culture of value creation. Having everyone do their own thing—a message that the inverted org chart could send—is antithetical to that.

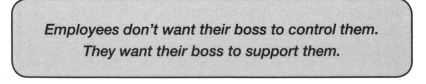

Employees don't want their boss to control them.
They want their boss to support them.

The challenge became how could we let people who are smart, creative, and inventive—people who want to be free to do their best work—contribute to our customers' success and still create a uniform approach for doing so?

Let's pause here for a second. You might wonder why we didn't decide to do what some companies do in this situation and simply tell everyone, "At all times, use your best judgment." Wouldn't that take care of the problem?

The answer is no, and there are three reasons why.

1. My best judgment may not be as good as yours, so you don't want to be using my best judgment. We want to rely on the judgment that will produce the best results for the customer.

2. The fact that you and I have differing standards of what best judgment is means we are not aligned, and that means we don't have a true corporate culture focused on creating value.

3. While we certainly want people to be creative, we don't want anyone to do something that could put either our clients or our company at risk. So we need some sort of rules or template we can all follow to ensure our behavior stays within acceptable bounds.

What this means is that an upside-down org chart is only going to work if everyone has—and adheres to—a common set of core values. We need to have a general understanding of how we will operate together, and the values provide that. If you don't have a common set of core values, then work could easily become a free-for-all and an unmanaged type of environment—and no one, not us nor our clients, will benefit.

These values create a commonality that helps form a strong bond between everyone in the organization, which gets all of us driving in the same direction.

HERE'S HOW WE THINK OF THIS

Early on at Coupa, we identified three values that we think are critical to making sure not only that we survive and thrive but that our customers do too.

Those three values are—

▶ Ensure customer success

▶ Focus on results

▶ Strive for excellence

It's about our customers, us, and how we will engage together.

Here's how we think of these values: They serve like guardrails on a hiking trail or the bumpers that they put in the gutters of bowling alleys during kids' parties (to keep the balls rolling down the lane). They are things that not only keep us out of trouble but keep us on the right path.

At the outset, everyone at our company agreed that these three core values would be our guiding principles (see "What Are You Organizing Around?"). Our strategy may change and so might our tactics, but these three things will remain absolute.

What Are You Organizing Around?

You get a new job at a new company, and you tell people, "I just joined this organization." Or you meet someone at a party and you say, "I'm a part of that organization." After you say that, you have to ask yourself, "An organization of what?"

And from a manager's perspective, what are you organizing? You're organizing people, right? So what are you organizing them around? Are you organizing them around daylight savings time? Are you organizing around the weather, around their interest in comic books, around their experience set? Probably not. But what is going to bring this diverse group of talented people together? Values: a set of common rules or norms that decide how an organization will operate every day, no matter what. That's what we decided to do—organize people around common values.

Here's how we did that. When our company was far smaller and we only had twenty-five people here, I asked all twenty-five what they thought our values ought to be. And then I reviewed all twenty-five answers, looking for commonalities. Then I proposed these three values to the group, and all twenty-five of us agreed.

Since then, every time we have taken a serious look at these three values, we've decided they are the right three, and we have kept them. By this point, I don't think we could change them. It's a binding force at our company. It is part of who we are.

Let's look at them in a bit more detail.

ENSURE CUSTOMER SUCCESS

This ties back to our discussion in chapter 2. We don't want to satisfy our customers—although it is nice when it happens—we want to do everything in our power to make them successful. The customer-success model aligns our interests with the interests of our customers in quantifiable ways. If the customer is successful, we are successful. That's why the wording *ensure customer success* is so important. It's not *consider customer success*; it's not *reach for customer success*; it's not *strive for customer success*. It's *ensure customer success*. In other words, no matter what, create a set of measurable, quantifiable value for the customer that they can raise a flag around (jointly with you) and say, "We've been successful." You want to achieve ongoing value creation.

FOCUS ON RESULTS

This follows logically from the first point. We firmly believe we are accountable to our customers to produce results. That is why achieving real, tangible, positive results is built into the DNA of our company and every employee and partner we work with. We see this as our most important responsibility, day in and day out: Produce results for our customers and produce results in all our efforts. You could focus on a lot of things, but your focus on a daily basis ought to be on producing some kind of result, making sure you are getting something done versus simply processing things.

STRIVE FOR EXCELLENCE

The idea is not to be excellent. And it is not, "Never make mistakes." It is about *striving* toward excellence, which recognizes that true excellence does not exist. There is no such thing as human-made perfection. But as long as you're consistently striving for it, even if you're making mistakes along the way, you'll constantly be getting better.

Striving for excellence is about never lowering the bar. Once they sign, too many customers have fallen victim to the blasé attitude and behaviors of their vendors. We strive for excellence by raising the bar for ourselves and for our customers. We constantly ask ourselves how we can be better than we were yesterday. That way of thinking ensures our customers are not only receiving great results but are getting the best we can offer on a day-to-day basis. We are constantly improving and innovating, which means our customers have the best product the market has to offer—bar none. And they can and should expect that they will continue to benefit from our continued quest for excellence. In the immediate future, this will be the standard that all customers will hold their vendors to.

"A man's got to have a code, a creed to live by."

—John Wayne

We think these three core values help build a culture that is best aligned with ongoing value creation. If you believe in these three values, you will do well here. If you don't, you won't.

Now, notice what is going on with these values. There is an internal element to them. It requires you—as an employee—to dig deep and say, "What does excellence really mean to me? Not just what's being demanded of me by the outside world. But what does it mean to me, in the context of helping customers succeed?"

This is by design. For example, when you ask millennials, the people born since 1980, how they think about their careers and where they want to apply their efforts for the next thirty-plus years, most of them will say they want to be involved with something that has some sort of purpose. They want their lives to be related to something that has a real meaning. They want to have the autonomy to express themselves purely and authentically. They don't want to be told what to do. They have access to all the information in the world at their fingertips. They don't want to be enslaved into something that isn't the best expression of themselves. If you, as an employer, are not supporting them during the forty to fifty to sixty hours a week of their life they are spending at work, then you're probably going to lose them to those that are willing to.

So if you want to attract, retain, and develop the best people so you can win in the marketplace, you need to think about supporting them by providing common guiding principles more than making them follow strict demands.

THIS IS NOT A ONE-TIME THING

You can't, of course, simply say once, "Listen up. Here are our core values," and then list them and expect them to take root. You have to talk about them time after time. You constantly need to overcommunicate them using different examples and different wording all the time, so that people internalize the values and make them their own. I promise you will be bored delivering the message long before anyone else is.

At every all-hands meeting at the company, every single one, I review the core values. And all of our performance reviews are based on the ways people express and adhere to them. That's what we review people on.

When we conduct an evaluation, the employee writes a self-review around how they've shown the ability to ensure customer success, focused on results, and striven for excellence.

How does this work?

For ensuring customer success, you might write, "I was the project manager on three customer deployments, and we met the measurable success criteria defined during the sale cycle. All three projects were completed within allotted time frames, they produced the margins we expected, and they came in within budget." Those would be things that ensured customer success.

For focusing on results, you might say, "I identified an inefficient process of communication between the professional services, product management, and support teams, and encoded, gained alignment, and rolled out a technology solution that improved communication inefficiencies by 50 percent." Or, "I improved speed of response time by 25 percent," or something like that.

And then for striving for excellence, your answer could be something like this: "After last year, when my best presentation was graded a 2.8 out of 5 at the annual conference, I worked hard on both my PowerPoint and communication skills and this year received a 4.3." You showed that you are striving to become a better presenter, and you've quantified the improvement you've made.

Your supporting manager would have an opportunity to weigh in on your responses to see if they saw it the way you did. Then, we stack rank employees in every department by those that delivered the most customer success, delivered the most results, and showed they were striving for excellence by trying to stretch themselves.

Based on all those criteria, we award bonuses, equity distribution, and compensation increases, and we decide who is going to get promoted. So these values—and the customer success that they produce—define a person's ability to earn more, get promoted, and take on more responsibility.

But we go even further: when it comes to our core values, our quarterly MVP awards are given to those who stand out in the way they exemplify our values. The MVPs are voted on by everyone in the company, so everyone gets to grade everyone else.

Here's how that works. Every three months, we send out a list of all employees in the company on a spreadsheet. And everyone in the company can anonymously write some commentary and rate their top three people, the ones who exemplified each of the three values. So you could end up nominating as many as nine people, three for each value.

We tabulate the nominations, and those who come out on top receive awards. This is another way of reinforcing that these values are important. Sometimes people get a trophy. In certain unique cases, we have given out up to $10,000 to take a vacation.

Not only do we want to reinforce the values, but we also want to thank people for doing what helps us as a company.

Our walls have the core values written all over them. We have them in the conference rooms. Plus, we have them on the reverse side of our employees' name plaques on their desk. On one side are their name, title, and a list of interests, and on the other side are the core values—so they always have them in front of them. In addition, a senior person copied on an email may respond, possibly company-wide, "Hey, what a great example of focusing on results, or ensuring customer success, or striving to achieve excellence." We let the entire company know when we see people living our core values.

And all of our customer presentations and investor presentations showcase our values.

The values define our culture. They permeate everything everywhere, and they're consistently reinforced through every method possible. That's probably the easiest way to say it.

Now, people sometimes misunderstand the values. That's inevitable, and it is okay. When they do, it is another chance for the leaders in the company to reinforce why the values are so important.

Let me give you some background to the story I am about to tell. In our company, we have a culture that includes a tolerance for making mistakes. For example, as we have seen, the third core value is to strive for excellence, and as part of striving for excellence, the idea is that it is okay to make mistakes if you learn from them. So "Take risks, but learn if you fall short" is part of our culture of striving for excellence. And we reinforce that culture by sharing mistakes openly among the group.

That's the background. Here's what happened: One of our guys, someone who is well educated, bright, and has accomplished a lot for us, was updating the group about a project he was working on for the management team. We love this guy. He is hard working and gets a lot of stuff done.

Because our values are so important, he was charting his progress on the project against all three: ensure customer success, focus on results, and strive for excellence. He got to the second core value, focus on results, and he had the word *status*. And in the column he wrote, "Spoke to VP of professional services in Europe about XYZ Company."

I stopped the meeting and said, "How is that a status, man? I talk to a lot of people all day long. I'm talking to you right now. You want me to put that on the slide? Just that you spoke to somebody doesn't mean anything to me. That's not a focus on results. Status, to me, is when something's moved forward, like for example, you and he agreed that this will be the next three steps to complete task four. Giving me a status report that says you talked to someone is not acceptable."

He saw the problem and understood it immediately.

When we had an all-hands meeting a few days later, I said, "Hey, do you mind if I share this example with the group?" And I wanted to because everyone loves this guy. But my point was to show that even the best of people sometimes get lost in process and forget to maintain a relentless focus on results. And that focus on results is what we value.

I did not make him look bad when I talked about it. I made him look good in the sense that here's the CEO putting him in the spotlight and showing how he's adhering to the third core value, which is strive for excellence, by getting better as a result of what he and I talked about. It was a chance for me to reinforce our values.

TAKING HOLD

How do you know the values have been internalized? It goes back to our earlier discussion of how people have to interpret them for themselves. You can't simply do this from the top down. You don't say, "These are our core values. Live them." You constantly showcase the benefits of the values so people buy into them on their own, because it makes sense for them. For example, most people want to get promoted. Well, if you work at our company, you see that the people who get promoted live our values. They help make our customers successful. Or they see that we have won business because of our values, and they make the direct connection between our values and our company's success.

So, as an employee, you come to understand that our values need to be a foundational element of your work and, in a funny way, a cultural norm. You get dressed in the morning. You brush your teeth. You eat breakfast, lunch, dinner. It's the same thing with our values. It becomes part of how you conduct yourself, simply because you see that the people around you are incorporating the values into their day-to-day work lives.

Now, there is definitely a self-selection process at work here. We talk about our values as part of the interviewing process, and we try to engage in a conversation about them. Often, people apply here because they hear about what we believe in and they find it like the proverbial breath of fresh air compared with where they are currently working. Or they agree that this is the way things are going in the future, and they want to be part of a company that's adopting those principles now rather than being forced into thinking about them in the future.

Other people hear about the values and they self-select out. They don't want to define their working life in terms of customer success. Or they need excellence defined for them. Or they are simply not assertive enough to have serious conversations with clients about what success is. They would rather do whatever the customer says and satisfy them, as opposed to helping them produce real value. These are the kinds of people that have self-selected out or have been asked to leave if we hired them by mistake.

This is true for senior managers too, by the way. Some people like the command and control structure of the typical org chart and refuse to join us. They enjoy the power they have in the traditional organizational structure, and they don't want to give it up. The upside-down org chart is a great qualifier or disqualifier of the type of management we want to have in our company.

Now, of course, people try to put their best foot forward in interviews, so they may say they totally endorse our values when they actually may not. So you look for proof.

Let's take a real example using the second core value, focus on results. This is the easiest one. Are there bullet points on the resume of the person you are interviewing that show what they have achieved, or what the team they were part of achieved? In sales, for example, people say things like, "I closed 250 percent of my quota." A programmer might say they coded this module, which resulted in a 25 percent productivity gain, or that they received the innovation award three years running in their current company. Those are the kinds of things you are looking for, instead of, "I led a team of people doing stuff somewhere." That's great. But the team might not have accomplished anything.

So you look for proof points of our three core values. For *strive for excellence*, can you see from their resume that they are growing in their career? Can you see a logical progression that shows that they were striving for something greater every year in their professional life?

HOW DO YOU KNOW THIS IS WORKING?

The ultimate test for whether you have built a value-creation culture is to look at your measurable success and ask if your company is flourishing.

▶ Are you taking market share faster than others?

▶ Are you doing things that are disrupting huge companies and reshaping your industry?

▶ Are you winning customers at a rapid pace?

▶ Are customers staying with you for longer than you had initially anticipated, or longer than they stayed with the competition?

In other words, you measure it in the business results of your organization. That's what leaders are accountable for in the end. They have to create a company that delivers. If you are doing that, you are probably on the right track.

You can see if you are creating value in other ways as well. Here's one of my favorite examples: There was a person who joined us in a senior position, someone who told me during their interview they would be extremely comfortable with our culture. They weren't. They were extremely political. They wrote tons of CYA emails and clung to a top-down reporting structure. On top of that, they would hoard information as a way of trying to make themselves more powerful.

And what happened was—and I was so excited about this— the organization did not let this person thrive. It was like the body rejecting an infection. The person became increasingly isolated and eventually left. This showed me the culture was self-enforcing and that the culture is going to kick out those who don't fit, cannot adapt, or cannot carefully help us evolve as a company.

When you have an organization that operates that way, and produces solid results for your clients, you know you are on to something good.

REWARDS

To make this work, you need to have highly differentiated rewards. You need to prove to people that the values are important and that if they live them, they will be rewarded appropriately.

At many companies, a person might be outperforming her peers by a factor of two or three, yet her compensation is maybe 5 percent more. That isn't right. Not only is it demotivating, it sends a message that you aren't serious about your core values. If your core values revolve around making your customers successful, and someone does that, they need to be rewarded.

At our company, if you are significantly overdelivering in terms of performance or showing a level of potential that's significantly above and beyond others, we're not afraid to have a differential of anywhere between 10 percent and 100 percent in total compensation compared to people in similar functions.

Some people, especially if they are not getting the higher compensation, might say it isn't fair. But it is extremely fair. To the person who is complaining, I would say, "Look, you are performing well. You are doing about what we expected. And the market rate for what you're doing is (let's say) $80,000 a year, and that is what we are paying you. If you weren't doing good work, you wouldn't be here. We would help you find another job. But you're doing well, and we thank you, and part of that thank you is paying you fairly.

"But the person next to you, who has a similar job, is producing at an exceptional rate, and because she is, we are going to pay her proportionally more. Over the course of the last year, if I look at what she's achieved, it's created substantial value for the company, and that is why we are paying her a significantly larger bonus amount. So, yes, we want a high differential. It doesn't mean you're bad, but it means she's exceptional. It also means that Joey down the hall, who was also making what you do but wasn't performing anywhere as well, is no longer here."

We are comfortable giving bonuses that end up being more than 100 percent of someone's base compensation, if they are extraordinarily productive.

TWO EXAMPLES OF THE VALUE CREATION CULTURE IN ACTION

Up until now, we have only talked about how the value-creation culture works internally. It only makes sense to show it in action (i.e., operating to help make customers successful).

Let me give you two examples.

As I have said, typically, companies try to satisfy their customers. They provide what the customer asks for, and if they do that successfully, they feel pretty good about themselves. If the product or service performs the way it is supposed to, and they can answer any questions the customer has, they believe they have done a great job.

In a value-creation culture, you want to take it a step further and make the customer successful. Satisfaction is nice but not truly necessary. Success is. And as I said, the way you make the customer successful is by sitting down with them and coming up with quantifiable business metrics that they and you need to achieve. In the process of doing that, you may help the client see that they have more opportunity than they thought.

That was the case in our work with Conway, the huge trucking and logistics company that is now part of XPO. When they became a customer, we did what we always do. We sat down and asked, "How do you define success? What metrics do you want to put into play?"

As we have talked about, that's a new conversation for many customers, one they aren't used to having. Usually, from their perspective, it's more like, "Look, I've already bought you. Just go away and let me use you." So, we have to assert ourselves and say, "Look, you did buy us. And we thank you for that, but we want to go above and beyond and help you achieve your business outcomes. Let's talk about how we can do that."

So we had that conversation with Conway, and out of it came the determination that they wanted to put $500 million worth of addressable spend through our system. We said great, and we got to work on that.

Now, there were some hiccups on both sides. They had some internal challenges getting buy-in from some of their people. Some people were reluctant to use the new program. That is always the case when you introduce something different. And there were some bugs on our end in integrating with the way they do business, and that hampered adoption as well. But at the end of year one, we were well on our way to solving the issues and hitting the agreed-upon goals.

At the end of the first year, we had put about $260 million through our system and Conway had saved $13 million. Most companies—the ones who are happy to just satisfy their customers—would have stopped there. But as I said, you shouldn't be aiming for customer satisfaction, and we don't either. So, we sat down and asked what else we could do to make them successful and inserted ourselves into their internal project teams. When we did, we discovered that they had $700 million a year they were spending on fleet maintenance that they were not pushing through our system. So we asked the basic question, "Why?"

They said, "Well, this is a complex spend category. It's attached to different systems, so we haven't really looked at that." So we asked the question again, "Why?" We continued to get deeper and deeper into it. Money is money, right? They were spending this $700 million, and there was a chance for cost savings. It turned out that figuring out a way to put that money through our system was easier than they thought. Then, all of a sudden, their goal went from putting $500 million through our system to $1.2 billion. From there, we added the $400 million or so that they were spending on fuel.

The more we talked with them, the more opportunities we found. For example, some 99 percent of their purchase orders are preapproved. By automating the payment process, we saved them about $10 per PO, or $1.1 million a year. And we did a similar thing with accounts payable, saving another $300,000.

This all came about because we kept pushing to find out what would make them more successful for our mutual benefit, as we partnered around a results-oriented approach.

There are two basic ways customers react when you start looking for ways to make them more successful. They can do what Conway did and say, in essence, "Thank you. We never thought of that." Or they can think that you are just trying to gain more revenues for yourself.

The first situation is easy, of course. Those customers intuitively grasp that there is money to be saved and you can help them save it. With the other reaction, we try to refer them to others we have done an extensive amount of work for, so they can understand the potential savings. And even that may not be enough. They'll say, "I understand the work you did for that other company, but things are different here."

So, we'll say, "Okay, we accept that it's different, but let's walk through it and create a baseline and see where we can improve things."

ANOTHER WAY TO MAKE THE CLIENT BETTER

The Conway story makes an important point. The kind of value disruption we are talking about is not going to happen overnight. You are not only going to have to quantify the value you provide each and every time right away; you are going to have to do it for a number of customers. You are going to have to prove yourself over and over again. You want to get to the point, where we are now, where potential customers can check with current ones to see if you actually do what you say you are going to do.

Having a positive reputation with previous clients helps you get business. Once you sign up a customer, and you have proven that you are providing quantifiable value, you have the right to assertively engage with them for more business. And why wouldn't they want to give you more? You've just shown them a return on invest-ment that's real.

Now, in the example involving Conway, we were talking about how we could improve a company's existing operations in order to make them more successful. But another way you can improve the performance of your customers is by helping change their existing processes to make them more efficient. You look to see whether everything is running on all cylinders. You ask these questions: Is everything set up correctly? Are there any areas of opportunity where they can save time, save some process pain?

In other words, you can serve as a consultant to them. And that is what we did with ServiceMaster, the Fortune 500 company, which also owns Terminix, Merry Maids, and Furniture Medic.

What we found was their approval system for expenditures was mind-boggling. There were seven hundred possible approval chains that could be followed, depending on the type of expenditure or the amount of the purchase. And, not surprisingly, there were remark-able inefficiencies. For example, in some instances, an invoice would be sent to the CFO approval group and then to the CFO himself who would, in essence, be approving it twice.

It was a management nightmare. Why was the approval process so complicated? Well, in this kind of situation, it is usually a carry-over from a previous system, a variation of the *this is the way we have always done things* discussion we examined earlier.

We simplified the process enormously to the point where now there are 30 possible paths, not 700+.

TAKEAWAYS

- ▶ A value-creation culture cannot be mandated from on high. The values need to resonate with your employees, who need to make them their own.

- ▶ You can expedite the creation of this culture by hiring only those people who have the traits you want to instill organization wide.

- ▶ The values need to be simple, clear, and constantly reinforced. Otherwise, they will never take hold.

WHAT'S AHEAD?

It is time to make the switch to providing value as a service, and the availability of data makes the switch easier than you might think.

CHAPTER 6

RIGHT HERE, RIGHT NOW: THE ROADMAP TO VALUE DISRUPTION

Hopefully, by now we've convinced you that value as a service is the natural next wave in business evolution. Here, we are going to tell you how to get in front of that wave, so you can ride it to greater success. The alternative is that you risk being swept away when it washes over you—as it invariably will—if you are left behind.

"Not so fast," you might say. "The economy is getting better. Orders are up and unemployment is down, and we are finally concentrating on growing our business instead of thinking about all the things we have to cut. Now doesn't seem to be the time I should be thinking about altering the way I do business. Why should I change now?"

There are four obvious answers. The first might be the biggest constant of all time: Things change. Yes, things might be fine now, but they won't always be. There is a reason we call them economic cycles (and not economic constants).

Second, change of any kind takes time, and the bigger your company, the more time it takes. Let me make an analogy. If you are riding a bicycle, you can move swiftly to your left fairly easily. It won't be instantaneous, but it will be quick. Steering a yacht? It takes a lot longer. A huge cruise ship? You need to start preparing even earlier.

You don't want to wait for your competition to make a change and then find yourself six months later struggling with how you are going to do it as well. You want to start early, because major transitions are difficult. Some fifty years after IBM said it wanted to move from selling hardware to being a services company, the transition still isn't complete. Things take time.

Third, as we know, being the leader—being the company that is first—gives you a hugely unfair advantage over your competition in just about everything. Leaders in any particular marketplace wind up gobbling up market share and getting greater margins. It's just a fact of economic life.

Finally, why would you wait? If our arguments so far are resonating with you, and you believe as we do that value as a service is the next stage in business evolution, then why not start now?

I know the next bit of pushback I am going to hear. It boils down to this: Change is hard. Therefore, the natural inclination, as we talked about earlier in the book, is to put it off until it is absolutely required.

> *Companies are more likely to get into trouble in good times than in bad ones.*

My reaction to that is this: By the time you decide you are ready to change, it may be too late. The competition may have already transformed the landscape, and you may have been disrupted to the point where you will be commoditized out of business. At the very least, your margins and market share will be significantly reduced, and the road back to greatness is almost always treacherous and completely uphill.

Remember Blockbuster? (Increasingly, people don't.) At its peak in 2004, Blockbuster had nearly sixty thousand employees and over nine thousand stores. Before technology became ubiquitous and broadband Internet connections were widely available, Blockbuster offered an intriguing value proposition. You could rent movies—both recent and classics ones—at a Blockbuster outlet nearby, take them home and watch them, and return them when you were done.

But the problems with Blockbuster's business model were obvious from the beginning. The amount of inventory—the movies and video games the chain rented out—was limited by the size of the store. Inventory management itself was tricky. (You wanted to have as many copies as possible of the hot movie when people came to rent on Friday or Saturday, but that inventory sat idle on less popular viewing nights, and eventually even hot movies cooled off and you were stuck with an awful lot of copies of *Addams Family Values*.)

Most troublesome was that you literally had to go to the Blockbuster store to pick out a movie—not knowing if your first choice was going to be available—and then you would have to go back to return it, incurring late fees—fees often far greater than the cost of the rental—if you didn't get the movie back in time. The entire process was remarkably inefficient and did not create a lot of value for the average customer.

It was clear early on that technology would upend Blockbuster's business model. But even when companies like Netflix and Redbox began gaining traction, and better technology made it possible for your cable or satellite company to rent you a movie with a click of your remote at home, Blockbuster was reluctant to change. They did not stay focused on the best path to customer-value delivery, and the rest is history. (And so is Blockbuster.)

By the time they tried to adjust in earnest, it was too late.

BUT WHY VALUE AS A SERVICE?

Hopefully, we have convinced most people that change is imminent, and it's better to prepare for that change earlier than anyone wants to. But the next bit of pushback is this: "Why must I change to value as a service?"

"I understand that I need to get better," you may say. "But couldn't I focus on things like technology or strengthening my balance sheet?"

Sure, but to what end? Are you making the technology better just for the sake of making it better?

Or, are you making it better to keep up with your competitors? In which case, you're playing catch up or you're further serving to commoditize what you have.

> *In the quest for getting better, I understand the inclination to keep wanting to go down the same path, by increasing the speed or quality of what you are doing. It is familiar and easier, even comforting. But the worst time to accelerate is when you are going in the wrong direction. Blockbuster would have still gone out of business no matter how efficiently it was run.*

Are you doing it because customers are telling you what they want, which may not always be what they need? (Think back to our Henry Ford quote: "If I had asked people what they wanted, they would have said 'faster horses.'")

Certainly, investing in technology makes sense, but you have to ask, to what end? If it is to build quantifiable value creation for your customers, then go for it. And if that requires you to strengthen your balance sheet by getting additional funding to get there, then that might make sense as well.

In other words, as long as your goal is to increase value creation for your customers (leveraging your company's core values), you may have a good strategy. But otherwise, you might be spinning your wheels.

The biggest reason you need to change toward this value-as-a-service approach may be the simplest: The demand for it is already under way. Let's take two radically different industries—automobiles and entertainment—to make the case.

HOW THE PROGRESSION WORKS

As we have discussed, the transition to value as a service has two parts. One component is demanding value, and the other is demanding it as a service. Customers in the general product world, and in more mature industries and more mature environments, are already unquestionably requesting value. With cars, for example, one value that people progressively expect is more miles per gallon (MPG), and indeed, the average MPG for all cars has been steadily going up.

The next step in the evolution will be electric vehicles. Once electric cars have gotten to a point where they are stable, reliable, and can go further on one charge, it is strictly going to be an economic decision when it comes to buying gas versus electric, all other variables held constant: "If I've got a twenty-mile commute every day and I take five trips with my family each year to our summer home, what is the ongoing cost for me to maintain and drive this electric vehicle versus one that's gas?"

With the move to value as a service in the automobile industry, we have seen the elimination of the need to own a car at all, as the rise of Zipcar, Getaround, and Uber shows.

There was a similar evolution in entertainment. Customers weren't particularly happy with cable and satellite companies. Their prices were high, and their service was legendarily bad. Therefore, alternatives cropped up, aided by the rise of enabling technologies like broadband Internet. We have already talked about Netflix, but now there are alternatives, like Amazon Originals, HBO GO, and several other promising entrants.

The initial battleground was what kind of increasing value you could provide in terms of movie availability—the time between a movie coming out in theaters and it being available in your home.

The next logical step was to eliminate the cable and traditional television networks completely, and we now have services like Apple TV and Hulu.

So the shift to value as a service is well under way, as the car and entertainment examples show. And the reason is because consumers are demanding it.

But this shift is not being driven only by consumers. Businesses want it as well. Look at advertising.

Let me give you a real example. I am sitting at home watching something on the Travel Channel with my kids. And during every commercial break it seemed I was shown an ad for a Tacoma truck. Over and over and over again, there was an ad for the Tacoma. I am not in the market for a truck; I'm never going to be in the market for a truck. Therefore, the value of that advertising that Toyota, which makes the Tacoma, is spending when it comes to me is zero. It's a complete waste.

Whereas, when I am on Facebook and I am looking at baseball-related sites, Facebook understands I am sports fan and knows where I live, and all of a sudden I am getting ads for San Francisco Giants merchandise or offers to buy tickets to a game. The value of that advertisement being placed in front of me is real, and it massively increases the likelihood that I would be interested in buying those Giants jerseys or whatever they are showing me. Advertisers want that kind of value, and that is why more and more ads are shifting to the web. Facebook is crushing the TV networks because they've figured out a way to get companies to advertise in a much more efficient and much more value-added way, with better value results. And they're able to quantify that for advertisers so much more easily than some vague, "Hey, forty thousand people watch this show, and they'll be exposed to your truck up to six times in the hour." Who cares about how many people see an ad if they are not interested in the product and never will be?

Here's another example, this one from an industry that you might have thought would not adopt value-as-a-service principles—aircraft engines on commercial airplanes. These engines are heavy, precisely engineered and manufactured machines. They weigh tens of thousands of pounds each, and they're built in the most traditional manufacturing shops in a highly process-driven environment and culture.

Yet the way these engines are marketed and sold is incredibly modern. The three big aircraft engine makers—General Electric, Rolls-Royce, and Pratt & Whitney—all offer various versions of *power by the hour* (i.e., a value-as-a-service business model where instead of buying the engine, customers pay an hourly fee every time the engine is in use).[2]

This model creates massive value for customers, because it gives them predictable operating costs over the engine's lifetime, which can be up to fifty years.

Instead of charging a huge sum up front—commercial aircraft engines can cost upward of $10 million each—to recoup manufacturing costs and charging for maintenance on top of that, these engine makers provide predictability as a service for their customers by giving them the engine and charging each time it is used. You have two of our engines installed on your plane flying from Boston to Tampa? It is a three-hour flight? You owe us for six hours of use.

Rolls-Royce was the first to introduce this model a couple of

2   http://knowledge.wharton.upenn.edu/article/power-by-the-hour-can-paying-only-for-performance-redefine-how-products-are-sold-and-serviced/

decades back, and the others followed suit quickly thereafter, because it created disruptive amounts of value for the customer.

Let's pause for a second here. Aircraft-engine manufacturing is an attractive industry with high barriers to entry, where every vendor enjoys healthy margins and has a fair amount of pricing power, and where the incentive to change quickly is low. If value as a service is front and center there, do we have any reason to believe that any other industry will evolve differently?

ONCE YOU DECIDE YOU HAVE TO CHANGE

Convinced you have to commit to the idea of providing value as a service, the question is how do you go about it?

Here's a possible ten-step approach:

1. UNDERSTAND YOUR COMPANY'S CORE COMPETENCIES.

Some companies are great technology companies. Some are great services companies. Some companies are great at innovation. Some are great production companies. Some are great logistics companies. But they are all good at some special thing. You need to understand what makes your company unique.

That, of course, requires a level of self-awareness as an organization, because any company anywhere could—in theory—do anything. It could focus on anything.

The question is this: What makes your company unique? You have to be relentlessly honest with yourself in coming up with the answer. In the case of Coupa, we are using modern technology to build intuitively usable products that create software solutions to complex business collaboration and internal workflow problems. So we apply that concept of usability and simplicity in prescriptive ways to all of our offerings. And that makes our software—and thus our offering—unique.

2. DETERMINE THE BEST MAPPING OF YOUR COMPETENCIES TO EXISTING AND EVOLVING MARKETPLACE, OR CUSTOMER, CHALLENGES.

You ask, "What does the world need that we are really good at? Are there problems that people have that we can solve with our unique competencies?" In Coupa's case, just because we know how to make usable, intuitive software doesn't mean we should try to apply it to the world of social networking. There is no problem there. Facebook is awesome and is very usable. So for us to spend our energy spinning up another social network probably wouldn't be a good use of our time. But applying our talents to arcane back-office technology solutions that were first created in the 1980s and 1990s? Well, that is another matter. That is a place where we can create a lot of value for customers.

3. DEVELOP A VALUE PROPOSITION THAT BEST LEVERAGES YOUR CORE COMPETENCIES AND THE OPPORTUNITIES IN THE MARKET.

You want to find the exact sweet spot between what you do best and where the biggest need is in the marketplace. In our case, we decided to focus on eliminating the real pain in a company's back office—cost control, compliance, and saving opportunities. And we used our strengths in usability, simplicity, and connectivity via the Internet to alleviate many of those challenges. We saw there was a lot we could do there. The mapping was strong.

4. QUANTIFY THAT VALUE PROPOSITION.

It is lovely that you think you have discovered a worthwhile value proposition in the first three steps. But it doesn't do you any good if you can't make money with it.

If we plan to spend our energy and money building up an R&D team that's going to be one hundred people, two hundred people, or three hundred people, and then putting a support staff around it, we need to know two things: (a) Do we think we will deliver sufficient value so that customers will be willing to pay us appropriately? In other words, if we are planning to charge them $1 million, will they save more than that from using us? (Otherwise, they will not hire us.) And (b) will we be profitable, charging that $1 million a year in subscription fees? Will that $1 million we receive be substantially more than enough to pay for the R&D and the services we provide so we can build a business that has good margins and long-term profitability?

The greater the gap between the value you can create and what it will cost for you to create it, the higher the likelihood that you are going to have a good long-term business that you can grow. The point here in step 4 is to see if you can build a business around what you think you have discovered in the first three steps.

5. TEST THAT VALUE PROPOSITION WITH YOUR CUSTOMERS.

Until this point, you have been making guesses—educated guesses to be sure, but guesses nonetheless—about whether you will find marketplace acceptance. Here, you begin to discover if you are right, by learning whether potential customers will buy from you. In other words, you start by literally asking them if they would be willing to pay you $2 million a year if you save them $10 million (or whatever your value proposition is). They will say yes or no, or they might say, "Yes, if you can overcome this particular challenge for us." You are looking to find the great gap in the marketplace that tracks to what you are good at, and then you ask people if they would be willing to pay you sufficiently to fill that gap.

6. ALIGN YOUR BUSINESS AROUND THE OFFERING.

If people are willing to pay you sufficiently for what you have to sell, you need to figure out the best way to design your organization to sell it. The starting point is easy: The entire organizational structure needs to be centered on optimizing the leverage of your core competencies and the value you can deliver to your customers. It's that simple. Then, the question becomes this: What's the best way to do it? You can organize around function, of course. Or you can organize around something else.

As you saw in the last chapter, at Coupa, we organize around our three core values of ensuring customer success, focusing on results, and striving for excellence. Obviously, how you decide to align your organization has all kinds of implications, ranging from the type of people you're going to hire to what you expect of them to how you take care of your customers.

7. REFINE EVERYTHING BASED ON CUSTOMER INPUT.

Confirmation that you are on to something is one thing. But the key goals of a business are to (a) get and keep customers and (b) turn a profit. So you want to be constantly fine-tuning your offering and your organization, based on what you hear from your customers. In our case, for example, early on, customers told us, "You have to be able to integrate your product into the Enterprise Resource Planning (ERP) systems that we have."

Initially, we thought that would be easy. We figured we'd use middleware that taps into everything, and we did. But we found that solution worked only for relatively small customers who didn't do anything too elaborate. We realized that when we got into larger accounts, we would have to build some of these things on our own, because it was the only way we'd be in a position to continue to deliver huge value to customers. They wouldn't be able to deploy our programs if we weren't able to snap into SAP and Oracle, for instance, in a configurable, flexible way. There wasn't anything on the market that did that, so we had to build it ourselves.

We refined our approach by building up an entire team of cloud-integration architects who built standard integrations to all the big ERP systems. If we hadn't done that, we would not have been able to service these huge customers in any way, shape, or form. We needed to refine our initial offering based on what our customers told us.

8. DEVELOP IT FURTHER AND FURTHER.

The point here is that you are never done. On a daily basis you need to be checking to see that you are growing properly and that you are providing real value.

Our move into invoice management is an example of what we are talking about. It wasn't something that we set out to do initially. But after we had been in business for a while, our customers began asking for it. We started in a small way, by tracking bills coming in. But as our customers asked us to do more and more, we began doing everything related to direct and indirect billing for products and services.

We've now processed hundreds of billions of dollars in invoices for companies around the world. But it only came about because we continue to evolve our product and bring our core competencies into areas that our customers ask us to handle, areas we had not anticipated at the outset.

9. MAKE THE CUSTOMERS PART OF THE SOLUTION.

Let me tell you a story to explain what I am talking about here. I was on a call with the chief information officer (CIO), chief procurement officer (CPO), and four other people from Sanofi, the $150 billion pharmaceutical company out of Paris. It was our biannual check-in. They told me everything was going great. They've deployed to thousands of users. They're leveraging their centralized contracts. They're saving money by using us. They have compliance. They're doing well. During the call, one of the people says, "Hey, obviously we're a big customer of yours, and going forward, we would like to be more involved in your roadmap design, planning, and all that. But at the same time, we absolutely want to only use standard product. We don't want you to design anything specific for us. We want only the best practices that you capture in developing the solution." That's a real partner. Because they are saying, "Look, we want to be a part of the solution with you, but we are also trusting you not to go off road and build some crazy thing that's only going to work for us, something that's not going to be upgradable in the future."

Why do we have that relationship? Because we made them part of the solution. We agreed with them that this platform we are developing is not just ours, it's theirs, too. We're taking a community-best-practices-development approach, and we're going to build something here that benefits us because it'll benefit a lot of companies. It'll benefit Sanofi because they'll have best practices encoded in it. (This is an example of what we talked about in "One Question *Not* to Ask Your Software-as-a-Service Vendor" in chapter 3.)

10. TRACK THE RESULTS WITH YOUR CUSTOMERS.

Yes, you've established the quantifiable success criteria up front. But after you have been working with a client for a while, it is not unusual for them to lose track of it, so we make sure we don't. We create dashboards that show customers how much they've saved using our products. It creates a team atmosphere, because it shows we are in this together. It also makes the client happy, because they can see progress.

SAY GOOD-BYE TO FLUFF

The more data and information that is available, the less room there is to hide. Too many companies—especially in the technology world—are used to selling on the sizzle, on the potential promise that they might provide. Those days are rapidly going away. Customers are increasingly demanding the steak.

A good example of what we are talking about is the group couponing sites like Groupon and Living Social. The sizzle was really great. "Look, by going through these sites, I can ride a horse for twenty dollars an hour in Sonoma, instead of the hundred dollars it usually costs." And so, lots of people signed up for deals like that . . . but few got anything of lasting value.

Yes, the stables got exposure, but so what? They lost money on every single ride. It probably costs them more than fifty dollars an hour, all in, to offer that ride. And there is no way they are going to recover that cost, if people don't come back and pay the full rate of a hundred dollars an hour, or close to it.

And yes, the people who were attracted by the twenty-dollar price got a good one-time deal, but again, so what? Groupon has trained them to pay below-market rates. They aren't going to pay full price in the future. They would feel like a fool. They would say to themselves, "Wait, I am now paying five times what I did for that initial ride? No way."

So there was a lot of sizzle but minimal steak at the end of the day. Some forty or even twenty years ago, it would have taken a long time for people to catch on to the fact that there wasn't a whole lot to it (i.e., there was little sustainable value) with the couponing sites. Today, things are different. Four years after Groupon went public, for example, the stock was trading at 10 percent of the price it did during the first day of its initial public offering (IPO). The initial model was not sustainable. A new team is now in charge, rethinking the future of the business.

Not only have we gotten better at measuring things—that is what analytics is about—but also, because of the Internet and the fact that the world is again flat, there is a rapid flow of information, which reveals things far faster. The Internet accelerates transparency. Think about the ratings on Yelp. If a restaurant screws up once or twice, it could immediately lose business, because the Yelp reviewers will let the world know. Somebody who gets a bad rating on Angie's List, which evaluates local businesses, is going to see the number of phone calls they get go way down.

> *You've got to have something backing up the promise that you are offering. If you don't, people will find out quickly.*

The easiest way to make the shift to value as a service is if there is no physicality to your product. If that is the case, you should be trying to convert your offering to a service or something that can be delivered on demand. People aren't going to want to own anything that can be stored in zeros and ones because they know it can be delivered as a service, like movies, music (and, of course, software), or any digital experience.

Let me give you a ridiculously simple example, which makes the point. Say your company makes a device that automatically converts Fahrenheit temperatures into Celsius and Celsius into

Fahrenheit—and the product works great. Even so, why would any-one want to own that today? If you type *What is 72 Fahrenheit in Celsius?* into the search bar in Google, the answer, *22.22*, pops up in 0.45 seconds. (Try it.) And if you speak the question into your smartphone, the answer comes almost as fast. (Thanks, Siri.) What's the value in having a product that does that? The company is in an analogous situation to Blockbuster just before it crashed. The product works great, but there are much more efficient ways to get the same payoff.

So what could the company that makes the temperature-convert-ing product do to provide value?

The Time Is Now for You Personally as Well

For people under fifty, the move to value as a service will be yet another in a long line of business initiatives that they will need to master. But by this point, people born after 1965 are used to ever-compressing product life cycles and more demanding customers and the fact that changes of all types—especially in business—are coming progressively faster. They get it.

The question is this: What do you do if you are older and don't want to change anything you're doing?

There are three options.

1. You can simply hope we are wrong in our belief that value as a service will become an important economic force soon. The problem with that approach is twofold. First, hope is not a strategy. Second, if you are betting against social or economic forces, invariably, you are going to be wrong. Just think about

all the change you have seen in your lifetime. That's why it's important to at least understand the long-term dynamics we're hypothesizing here.

2. You can simply retire, if you have enough money. (But, as the crash of 2008 showed, people who thought they would never have to work again ended up going back to work once the value of their retirement accounts dropped dramatically. You never know what is going to happen in the markets.)

3. You can adjust. I understand that this is probably not important to you, if you work in the cable industry and you're planning to retire in three years. But if you want to have a career that extends at least five more years, you probably ought to consider altering your approach, because you don't want to be laid off. Or you don't want to be caught in a slow-growth company, or no-growth industry, that is not going to allow you to personally thrive.

Well, the device could deliver the information in real time. When I exit my bedroom, I could ask out loud, "What's the temperature outside in Fahrenheit?" and it would give me the answer. Or when my wife walks out and says, "What is the temperature in Celsius?" it could provide that answer as well. Or the device could already know my preference to hear the temperature in Fahrenheit and for my wife to hear it in Celsius, and if someone else asked the question, it could give the number both ways, so they don't even have to think about saying Fahrenheit or Celsius. The value would be that we'd receive that information instantaneously, at point of need. There would be no products to search for—where did I leave that darn converter—or conversions to do by hand or with a calculator. You could bundle it into a Nest thermostat or any of the other electronic products that you can use to run your home. That way, the product would be delivered in a way that drives value for me.

Now, again, the maker of the product may be initially resistant to these ideas. They have always made a product that they have sold to retailers. And they'll say that they really don't want to change what they have been doing. But the fact is, no one is going to buy it anymore. The dollar store is filled with things that have become useless. The things you see there are über-commodities. In fact, they are beyond commodities. They are like celery. When you chew celery, you don't consume calories; you burn them because celery is so difficult to eat. It's the same thing with the items for sale in the dollar store. The market has decided that these products provide negative value. Your time and energy are much too valuable for you to spend money on a product like the Fahrenheit-Celsius converter.

There isn't much of a market for things like this anymore. For example, if you are going from New York to Chicago and you want to figure out the best way to do it, AAA has a service called TripTik. You can write to them, and they will send back a map with the route marked. Everybody from Google Maps to MapQuest to Waze has figured out a way to provide that in real time and make money while doing it. There is no longer a reason to send away for a marked-up map. (And, indeed, AAA is now providing this service online. It was forced to change, but they probably did so later than they wanted to, in hindsight.)

What this underscores is a point we made in chapter 1. Many product companies are in the process of converting their models to service-type businesses, and in the context of doing that, they should be considering the next step, which is the value they'll be delivering as a service. Simply converting from up-front payments to a subscription model won't bring you into the modern era, if you're not providing value.

DON'T STOP THINKING ABOUT TOMORROW

When you start down the road to value creation, you not only want to be focused on value creation today, you want to be prepared for the future as well. For example, at Coupa, we're capturing a lot of transactional-spend information. We know what companies are buying from whom and at what prices, how quickly they're getting it delivered, how often they're getting invoiced, which suppliers are liked and disliked, and much more information.

Over time, we're getting a whole host of data so that in the future, we'll be in the best position to offer our customers greater value, such as prescriptive advice on who they should be working with, what prices they should use as a starting point for the negotiations, and suppliers who follow green practices.

> *In terms of value creation, you don't want to only think about today, but also about putting in place a platform, infrastructure, and ecosystem that will allow you to extract or deliver more and more value for customers tomorrow as well.*

Benchmarking works in the exact same way. We not only collect data from individual customers, we are also collecting data across all customers. So we're now able to create value for customers by benchmarking them against their peers. For example, we will tell you that, in your company, it takes three weeks to approve the purchase of a laptop, but across the network of millions of users and hundreds of companies, the average is seventy-four hours to get something like that approved, and the approval goes to two people, but in yours, it goes to ten. So perhaps your constructs are too tight. Or you're too restrictive. Or you're too bureaucratic. And this might suggest that maybe you should allow self-approval up to $200 and maybe have two people signing off on a laptop, instead of ten. We can show you where you stand, which is always a good concept. It's like sports. For example, you know you are running a ten-minute mile. But is that good? Bad? Average? You don't know until you compare that time to others.

In the enterprise software industry, big-data analytics and machine learning are in their infancy. We're looking forward to driving even more value for our customers by employing these developing constructs.

TAKEAWAYS

- ▶ The move toward value disruption is inevitable. You either start making the move to value as a service now, or you run the risk of being left behind.

- ▶ The transition will be made much more efficiently if you follow the process we laid out earlier in the chapter—the one that begins with understanding your company's core competencies and ends with tracking the results with your customers.

► As you make the transition, make sure you are preparing for tomorrow as well as today.

WHAT'S AHEAD?

If we all need to provide more and more quantifiable value in the near future, we are going to need to create more and better metrics to track how well we are doing. That's the subject of our next chapter.

CHAPTER 7

THE RISE OF NEW VALUE MODELS

I t's time to reevaluate how you evaluate. That is the clear takeaway from everything that we have talked about until now.

Before, you were focused on delivering a good product or a reliable service, meeting deadlines, turning a profit, and the like. All those things are still important. But they will need to move down a notch on your priority list. Making sure your customer is successful must be at the top.

What follows is that you need to reevaluate the way you market: You need to reevaluate your culture and what you believe to be your company's core competencies—in short, all the building blocks of your organization—to make sure you are concentrating on your customers' success.

You have no choice.

I know that some of you are still saying, "I don't have to change. My company is never going to be in the situation that Blockbuster was, and we certainly don't make a product (or provide a service) as simple as the Fahrenheit to Celsius converter that you talked about in the last chapter. We're different."

You may be. But our guess is the people who are finding themselves left behind by the transition to value as a service said the same thing before the competition passed them by. That's why, in the previous chapters, we provided various tools and ideas you can use to help make the transition.

With that as background, let's talk about how you want to operate going forward, and to fully understand that, some context will help. Let me start with our industry, because I think it is representative of what will be happening everywhere fairly soon.

If you were a company like ours in the enterprise-software space, customers used to see you merely as a vendor that they could plug in to solve a problem.

Here's how it would work: Customers had something they were wrestling with, and they would hire us to provide a technological solution. In that kind of relationship, they would evaluate us on the features we could provide, how quickly we could provide them, and at what cost.

But in the new value model, the customer won't be interacting with us that way, asking if we have this feature or that one. They'll be looking for us to be business partners. They'll say, "Okay, we understand you're going to bring forth these capabilities, but ultimately, what we're agreeing on is the value you're going to deliver for us, and as long as you deliver that value for us, we don't care how you do it."

It's like the guy who cuts your lawn. You could send him a request for proposal (RFP) to look at how good his lawn mower is. Are the blades sharp? Is it well oiled? Is it a Yamaha or some other reliable brand? You could kick the tires.

Or you could say, "I don't care about any of that. How the landscaper gets the job done is his business. He can use scissors and personally cut each blade by hand if he wants to. We have agreed that he is going to keep the grass between one-half and three-quarters of an inch high and that there will be no bare spots on my lawn greater than one inch in diameter. That's how I will judge him. That's the value I am paying for. I am not paying him to come twice a month, whether the lawn needs to be cut or not. I'm not paying because he is a good guy and has been working for me for years. I'm paying him for the value of whatever it is we have agreed on." That's the new model.

People won't be selling products or services because the products or services are a means to an end. They'll be selling the ends (i.e., the result). They'll be selling the measurable outcome. In the case of the lawn guy, it is that he will keep the grass at the agreed-upon length.

This is going to be a major change in how sellers are judged. And the change on the buyer's side could be just as severe.

Let's take the typical business, for example. Today, most companies are being judged based on whether they're profitable. And making a profit is important. They are also being judged on their rate of revenue growth. That's important, too, because in today's environment, if you are not growing, you are shrinking and will eventually fade away. Another measure of success is how much you are spending on sales and marketing. That's important because potential customers need to know you exist. Yet another measure is operating margins, which are also important. How quickly can you get to positive cash flow? That's important, too.

But as things evolve toward a customer-success orientation, an entirely new set of ways to evaluate companies will emerge. For example, customer retention rates will become more crucial as an indicator of company health. Yes, they are being evaluated now, but it is sort of an afterthought to the other key areas mentioned. It will be extremely important going forward. Another customer-success metric might be your net promoter score. In the case of our lawn-mowing friend, this is essentially the percentage of his customers who are willing to recommend his services to a colleague or friend minus the percentage who would actively discourage others from using his services. This is a great way to quickly measure the health of your customer relationships.

But the ultimate metric will be the success criteria that you define with your customers. In this way (in the case of business to business), even if your purchaser leaves the company, the results against the success criteria stay, and that is the best possible defense against churning customers.

But it's not necessarily that we are going to look for new metrics. It's more than possible that we will look at existing metrics in new ways. For example, today, if your sales and marketing costs are extremely high and you're extremely unprofitable, most people will have little confidence in your company. Investors will be hard to come by.

But if a company is able to clearly articulate how they're creating a certain undeniable value set for their customers, and their product is delivering, and the customers can validate that, there might be greater conviction. There might be greater confidence. There might be a greater interest in the financial markets to get behind companies that have these attributes.

> *In the future, you may look at different metrics to evaluate your business, and you might be looking at existing metrics differently, based on how you think business will evolve.*

Some fifteen or twenty years ago, Amazon would have been a good example of what we're talking about, because they had been unprofitable forever and their sales and marketing costs were absurd. But good investors saw the value creation in what the company was doing. They understood that Amazon was providing an amazingly broad selection. They were giving you speed of delivery. They were providing ease of use, so it saved time. They built their core competencies around those value propositions and delivered on them. The next question for investors was, "Could it scale?" And it could. So you could have used different metrics to evaluate Amazon, and if you had, you probably made a lot of money investing in their stock.

Examples of evaluating companies differently are starting to happen all around us. Take business process outsourcing, which is a huge trend. It's where companies take a certain part of their operations—like human resources or their call centers—and turn them over to an external vendor to run. The company and vendor agree on certain specs. The vendor will provide a certain agreed-upon level of customer satisfaction via the call center response time, for example, or they're going to ensure this level of accuracy for the company in its employee-benefits distribution and its payroll, paychecks, and tax filing for employees.

The vendors are selling business value—"We promise to deliver this level of quality for this price." They are not selling a product. It's no longer, "This is what we offer, and this is what we charge." It's a conversation about the value that you as the buyer are looking to attain. It's also about what your challenges are and whether they map to what the seller is good at and whether you can work out a price that both sides can live with.

The shift to value as a service is under way.

> *In some industries, continuing to sell products will not work. Enterprise software is one of those industries.*

You can see where this is going. Think back to the Facebook example that we used in the last chapter. In the future, Facebook is not going to charge for the number of people who see an ad or click on an ad. The ads will be free, or at least, they will be at a low cost. Facebook will likely make its money by getting a percentage of every sale made from someone who is on the site, clicks on an ad, and buys something as a result. The final frontier will be paying for measurable value, which in this case, is revenue to the advertising companies.

It is more than possible that every company will move to this *risk-sharing* model. I call it that because the arrangement will have risk on both sides. In the past, the client—the person paying for a product or service—was taking a risk because they never knew for certain if the purchase would provide value for them. Even if it didn't, they were still out the money.

In the model we are discussing, there is risk on both sides. If the vendor doesn't provide the agreed-upon value, then they won't get paid.

To see how this could play out, let's go back to our discussion about business-process outsourcing and the decision to turn the call center over to a vendor. The risk for the business is that they are outsourcing control of a key business function—the call center. But there is risk for the vendor as well. It will no longer be a guarantee that the business, their client, will pay anything (or at least not much) for the day-to-day functioning of the center. The business could say, "It costs us $10 million a year to run the center. We will pay you $7.5 million, which we figure is the actual cost."

Why would the vendor take the deal? It could be because of this: Both sides could agree that the real value revolves around customer renewals. Let's say I'm T-Mobile, and I have a call center that manages customer escalations, the term for when a customer is likely to leave. Well, right now, every time one of those escalation calls goes to my call center, 50 percent of those callers end up leaving.

However, if you, the vendor taking over the call center, can improve that by 50 percent—so the number of people leaving drops to 25 percent—I will give you half the money I receive by keeping those additional customers. I will split the money with you, and just to make up a number, your share might be as high as $50 million annually. All of a sudden, managing the call center at cost seems like a better deal.

Risk Sharing: Simple but Potentially Not Easy

Risk sharing makes a lot of sense, and I am absolutely convinced it will be one of the models that catches on as we move to value as a service. However, there are three things to guard against.

First, when you move toward any kind of sharing model, it's hard to get it to work until you know you can trust the other party. That's the number-one thing people are going to worry about: Trust. It's wonderful if you have an existing relationship and you have built up that trust over time. But if it is not there from the beginning, you have to build it.

One of the ways you create it initially is, as the old saying goes, you *trust but verify*. You monitor one another, which is, of course, one more reason to understand what the heck you're measuring. If you're saying our partnership revolves around value as a service, you need to know what the value is and how both parties are going to measure it, to make sure that each side is performing as promised.

What is the second potential problem? You will have a natural inclination to try and minimize your share of the risk, while also trying to optimize your share of the reward. That's why we need to have crisp clarity on the metrics and a way to track them, so that everything is transparent. That way, it is far easier to strike a deal that is fair to both sides.

The final problem is that one side may think there is too much potential for the other.

Let's go back to our call center example. If the vendor says, "Let's split whatever I save you." (This could be as much $100 million in the call center example.) The client might say, "I'm not ready to write you a $50 million check. But I could see going as high as $5 million."

To which the vendor's response might be, "If you are only willing to pay me $5 million of the potential savings, then you better be willing to take on some risk, and you better pay me $2.5 million up front, which I get no matter what. In this instance, our upside is limited as a vendor, but at least the downside is limited, too. We're guaranteed that $2.5 million."

All these potential difficulties can be resolved. I wanted to present them to underscore that while the idea of risk-revenue sharing makes sense, it is not an automatic slam dunk.

So basically, you're in business with me now. You're an extension of my company. Your job is to get these customers to not leave, and only if they don't do you get paid. If they all keep leaving, if you don't improve my metrics, I am not paying you anything.

It's a true risk-sharing model, and we have employed it from time to time at Coupa. We have gone to potential customers and said, "If we don't save you X dollars in the next Y months, you only pay us a fraction of X. But if we save you X dollars or more, you pay this much more"—and the more was a percentage of what we saved them. It really was savings as a service.

We're not doing that full time yet, but we are moving toward it. It is the best way to stand behind what we offer our customers. We've still got a lot of work to do to automate and streamline on both ends, but that's the direction we're contemplating taking our business going forward, because otherwise, I can't stand behind my offering to you.

> *Risk sharing forces value orientation. At some point, when you start arguing about how much value you can deliver, the client is going to say, "Well, prove it." And then you engage in a risk-sharing discussion, which is good for everyone.*

Since we are so early in the process, we don't know what a definitive list of potential value options might be. But we can take a guess at some of them. Vendors might be paid for increasing a company's client-retention rate or helping improve their image in a measurable way or some other metric. It is easy to come up with an entire list, which underscores the high likelihood that this is going to happen. The forward-thinking companies that come up with these new models will be ahead of those that don't.

But let's be clear: you're going to be forced into this new way of business, no matter what. Our message throughout has been that change is under way; therefore, you need to think of everything you do in terms of providing value as a service.

How long will the transition take? My guess is that it is going to be like any other major business or societal change. There will be resistance at first, but once the idea gains momentum, it will take hold with remarkable speed.

Take the profit-sharing arrangement in the hypothetical T-Mobile example. I don't think our customers at Coupa are yet ready for something like that. I don't believe the category is mature enough to appreciate this approach. The change would happen too fast. People in our industry are still trying to get their heads around the shift from products to services, which is what we're experiencing right now. So for us to immediately begin discussing being paid by a percentage of savings created is something our customers—for the most part—are not prepared for. It would be too big a leap. I'm not sure there are many boards of directors out there who would be comfortable with their CEO saying, "For the next three years, we're only doing risk-share models."

> *We have no idea what types of value models will appear over time. But we do know the greater the precision around the value being delivered and the greater the ability to track it, the more options you will have. You will pick the measure that tracks best to your core competency.*

The board's response is likely to be, "Wait a minute, we have a core business here. Are you sure you suddenly want to leave the reservation and do something as risky as that, even if it's the future?"

Some things have to take their natural evolution. You can't skip a step; you need to have forward-thinking people who spend their days open to new ideas and concepts. Generally, society doesn't function that way.

The landscaper is a great example of the challenge we would be up against to make that move now. Let's use me as an example to further illustrate the point. Today, I would be at the point where I would let the kid down the block cut my lawn. But because I recently had experience cutting my own lawn, I am going to check out the mower the kid has and make sure he knows what he is doing before I hire him. For me to get to the next level, the starting point in our relationship should be that the grass is always between one-half and three-quarters of an inch high, and I don't care how he does it. Today, it would be too much of a mental leap for even me.

You have to be aware of a human being's natural resistance to change as we go through this transition. Otherwise, the process would be a lot faster. People are slowing it down.

But the change will occur, and one of the major reasons it will is that people don't have time anymore—and they will have less and less time in the future.

Better Metrics Will Make Value as a Service Easier

One of the reasons that risk sharing, in whatever form it will take, will widely come about is because it will be easier to see. The access to more data, and the creation of more metrics around value, will open the window for more risk-sharing models. It will support the change and encourage it to happen.

Let's go back to the lawn example, and let's say, for the sake of argument, that you agree to pay the landscaper a slight premium over the going rate if he keeps your lawn between one-half and three-quarters of an inch high, but you and he also agree that if he fails to do that, you will only pay him 50 percent of his going rate.

Suppose every day thereafter, you can not only look at the lawn with your own eyes, but there is also a little gauge on your mobile phone that shows exactly how high the grass is, and the gauge keeps track of that growth over time. Or imagine you subscribe to an alert sent to your smartphone that tells you the moment the gauge shows the lawn creeping above the agreed-upon length.

You could show the landscaper the graph, which would reveal that, over the last year, your lawn has been four inches high in certain months and a quarter inch in others. Either he cut it too short, or you had a jungle. He did not live up to the agreement, so you are only going to pay him half his going rate, or some other percentage of payment based on the measured result.

Conversely, if he keeps it within the range you and he agreed on, you are more than happy to pay the premium.

The metrics, and the ability to track them, make this relationship possible.

Gone are the days where you had the time to order something in the mail, wait four to six weeks for it to arrive, take out a big owner's manual, and read every page in order to get something to work. The rate of human interaction and information sharing is so accelerated today that simplicity and time are at a premium. That is what will drive this change.

I can't think of any industry—from medicine to financial services to retail—that won't be affected.

> *Every business should be considering value-as-a-service models, even if they sell products.*

Let's deal with retail. How might it work? Well, it already is. Consider a company called the Trunk Club. You, the customer, complete a style survey and they connect you to a person who will find the best clothes for your size, style, and preferences. As it says on its website: "Your stylist will hand pick a selection of clothing and send you a preview online. After you review the items, your trunk will be shipped straight to your door. Take ten days to try everything on, and then keep what you like and send the rest back. Shipping is free both ways, and you can request a new trunk anytime you'd like." There is no minimum purchase.

Now, compare this with your existing alternatives. You go to a store where you may not find anything you like, or even if you do, the store may not have your size, and even if they do, you may try it on later at home and change your mind. Now, it's time for another trip to the store and then to another store, so you can do this all over again. Doesn't this remind you of how we used to interact with Blockbuster? To make the point even stronger, this is a situation where there actually is a real, must-have physical component to the product being provided (shirt and pants versus streaming video). What happened to Blockbuster—and every other inefficient, less-than-value-optimizing business model—is occurring in every industry today, and this transformation will continue to work its way through every sector in our economy.

DIFFERENT JOURNEYS TO SAME DESTINATION

As the previous discussions show, moving to new value models won't be a one-size-fits-all approach. Different companies, even within the same industry, will come up with different approaches.

One reason for that will be because even though product life cycles are accelerating, they are still moving at different speeds depending on what you do for a living. Think back to Henry Ford and what he said about the Model T—you can have it in any color you want, as long as it is black. How long was it until cars changed dramatically? It took a couple decades before we had the level of customization and specificity that produced things like sports cars, different colors, and different styles. The industry probably did not flourish till the 1950s, with what are now considered classic cars that came out of Detroit.

In contrast, look at cell phones. How long do we have to wait for dramatically new options, sizes, and shapes? It is only one or two years at most. It's much like Moore's Law: Things change at an ever-accelerating pace.

The same dynamic will play out with value as a service. In the early days, the value may be as simple as saving you money (i.e., grabbing the low-hanging fruit, as it were). But over time, when everyone does that, you will need to move on to something else in order to stand out.

Think back to our lawn example. You might be the first to offer keeping the grass between two levels of agreed-on length, between one-half and three-quarters of an inch, let's say. But you can imagine, over time, your competition will start doing that, so you will need to create another level of differentiation. You might agree with your customer that value also includes keeping 95 percent of the grass greener than the average in the community, with less than five two-inch-diameter bare patches per two hundred square feet. These value constructs could then be included in bundles for your customer to choose from, such as bare-minimum maintenance, keep up with the neighborhood, and lawn-care rock star. But, underneath, there will be complete clarity on the value-as-a-service metrics being committed.

There'll be a whole personalization element that develops, and if you're value oriented, you will be able to move more quickly to incremental value delivery, which—for our lawn guy—might mean cleaning up the leaves under the bushes and keeping the trees trimmed. Or it could mean planting new shrubs and keeping things from growing on the fence, if your competitors match you on the idea of keeping 95 percent of the grass green with less than five clearly delineated bare patches.

A whole world of value-creation opportunities opens itself up when you start engaging with a customer in a value-oriented way rather than saying, "Hey, I've got this product, would you like to buy it?"

There are two ways of looking at this. One is if you are providing value as a service, your work is never done. There's always more value that can be created, because (a) your competition has matched (or will match) the product or service you are offering, so you need a new way to differentiate yourself, or (b) there are always going to be more things that your customers will want.

But here's the more positive way of looking at this. If you move to value as a service, the growth potential for your company becomes unleashed, and you will have the opportunity to make a lot more money, because you're going to get paid for doing all that additional work. It's not like you are just doing favors for somebody.

The lawn example is a great one. If the same landscaper who was providing value to you by keeping the lawn between one-half and three-quarters of an inch high came to you—after doing exactly what he had promised for three months—and said he wanted to talk to you about taking care of your trees and shrubs as well, why wouldn't you consider his proposition? You'd be open to it because you share a common language, a language of measurable value creation, of quantifiable value.

He doesn't have to pitch you on the new weed trimmer he bought or the quality of his hedge clippers. You no longer care about that, because he has proven to you the quality of the work he does with the lawn. You're in a whole different world; you don't need to hear the sales pitch because you guys are speaking numbers and value now.

There's a common language that develops around metrics. We start talking about specific things. It is not about doing a good job. It's about keeping the grass three-eighths of an inch high or the call center retaining 25 percent more customers. The result is that the interaction between buyer and seller becomes operationally more efficient. This common language is extremely precise when it comes to what businesses do every day.

What do businesses do? They generate revenue. They drive profits and pay people in the process. And they buy things and add value to them and sell them. All of these activities are grounded in numbers. They're grounded in money in some way. Businesses are processing goods and services and creating money that they can use to buy more goods and services and to give back to investors. Everything is quantifiable. So if the value propositions themselves are also articulated in that way—if the lawn guy promises to keep the grass at a certain length and guarantees no dead spots—it's the most operationally efficient way to interact with you, and it will likely result in you giving him more work.

Now, there is a subtlety here. People could say to me, "Come on. All you are really saying is if a guy does a good job, you'll give him more work." That statement is certainly true. But I'm saying it's much more than that. We are now speaking a common language of quantifiable value and real metric delivery. It is clear what both sides are receiving, and the relationship becomes optimized. As you know, the phrase *good job* is notoriously subjective and uncertain, and there is often a lack of alignment between the person saying it and the person hearing it about what *good job* means. That problem goes away when you are speaking a common language rooted in numbers.

Perhaps there is no clearer example of the rise of new value models than companies like Solar City, which helps homeowners capture the sun's energy to power their homes. Companies like this have totally changed their marketing approach. In the early days, these companies would spend all their time talking about how solar was good for the environment, and they might mention that you could get a tax credit of some sort by installing solar panels.

Now, it is strictly about saving money. On Solar City's website, there's language like "Get control of your energy costs with America's number 1 solar provider," and you get "a production guarantee at no additional cost." Heck, they even have a calculator you can use to see how much money you can save on your monthly energy bill. The entire pitch is 100 percent value orientation. There is nothing else to discuss.

As long as I can get over the fact that I'll have a bunch of solar panels on my roof, which will make my house look less attractive, and I can get past the hurdle of having to talk to someone for a couple of hours as they try to sell me, the value proposition for me as a buyer is really pretty simple. I am spending $300 a month on electricity now. And when I install the panels, it will be $200 a month, so I will be saving $100 a month. Then the calculation moves to how much it will cost to put up the panels and how long they are going to last. The math is crystal clear. I will invest or not, taking into account the time value of money. It's easy to get to a value equation.

For the solar panel companies, the focus is now around highly efficient sun-energy capture and low production costs. It took a long time for those companies to get to a place where they could define a value-oriented message that was strong enough to overcome the control that traditional energy companies had around distributing energy to your house and to get past the natural skepticism that many potential buyers had. But they've got it down now. It's all about saving money. There's virtually nothing else in their message, and frankly, nothing else is necessary.

Overnight Success, Seven Years in the Making

You have probably noticed an interesting phenomenon as we have talked about the evolution to value as a service: It is not linear. Things do not smoothly transition from one delivery model to the next.

That isn't surprising. In Silicon Valley, there is this accepted idea that every overnight success has been seven years in the making (i.e., there is a tremendous amount of hard work that goes into something before everyone recognizes it as a success, seemingly at the same time). And what's also true is that at times, competing models wrestle for dominance with each other—one may be ascending in popularity while the other is on its way into obscurity.

We have people demanding more and better gas mileage from traditional cars, and yet we see that car ownership is down with millennials, some of whom rely exclusively on Uber and Zipcar—the next evolution in value as a service in automobiles. The cable and satellite companies are now adding more features, benefits, and even original programming, while simultaneously, people are cutting the cord and going network or cable or satellite free.

continued on next page

The reason this dichotomy exists is simple. As we have talked about, people and companies don't like to make radical changes, and some people adapt to changes earlier than others. (Eventually just about everyone gets there. When was the last time you saw someone using an abacus?)

Take cars, for example. Initially, all I could do was buy a car. Then I had the additional option to lease it, which is another way of saying I could rent it for X months for a fixed price. Then I could use Zipcar, which is a situation where I have access to a car as a service. I only use the car as much or as little as I'd like and pay per use.

But you could make the argument that companies like Uber are a step beyond Zipcar and are beginning to touch the bounds of value as a service by saying, "I don't want to own or lease a car or even be involved in driving one. What I want is the service of being reliably and expediently driven from here to there."

And I think we will go beyond that. I could imagine BMW saying, "For $10,000 a year we will give you a 5 series car with every cost included—insurance, gas (we will give you a prepaid credit card), maintenance, and so on—and then at the end of the year, you turn the car in, and we will give you a new car, one that has just rolled off the assembly line, the one from the next model year, if you renew your subscription."

It would be like the phone companies that promise you the newest phone as soon as it comes out, if you go with their plan. If it works with phones (and it's popular) why not with cars?

Will every consumer migrate to this kind of model, immediately? No, but some will leave Lyft and Uber to do it. And as everyone moves up a notch, the bottom offerings will fall away. Need proof? Once upon a time, people were happy with Model T Fords that they could have in any color they wanted, as long as it was black.

You can see this sort of idea taking place in municipalities as well. There are small towns where there is no trash pickup. You have to take your garbage to the dump. You used to pay a flat fee and drop off all you wanted. The municipalities tried to encourage more recycling—which, of course, would reduce the amount of trash they had to handle—but they didn't make much progress. It was like the solar companies initially trying to sell you on the benefit of going green. Everyone nodded and said it was a good idea, but few people did anything about it, because there was never a true value proposition.

Like the solar companies, the municipalities figured out a different approach. Many of those towns have switched from one flat annual fee to charging by the number of bags thrown away. All of a sudden, trash collection is down, because people understand exactly what throwing the trash away costs—and recycling and composting have gone up.

TAKEAWAYS

▶ If we are going to create a new way of doing business, we need to create new value models to ensure our customers are successful and we all make money.

▶ These models will evolve and come to the fore over time,

but they will all probably contain two features: Buyer and seller will be partners in some form, and how the seller is paid will reflect that.

▶ Companies are not all that far along on migrating to value as a service, and part of that is because of change-management issues. As we have said, people resist change. When people think of things one way, they get stuck in that way of reasoning. But the change is clearly coming, and when it happens, it will occur far faster than people might imagine.

WHAT'S AHEAD?

We will sum up what we have learned so far and give you a chance to tell us if we have practiced what we have preached and provided you with value as a service.

CHAPTER 8

CONCLUSION: WHAT
WE HAVE LEARNED

We have covered a lot of ground. But that isn't surprising, given how quickly the business world has been changing.

Think back to the early days of the enterprise software industry. As we discussed in chapter 3, a vendor would produce a product—maybe it would work fine, maybe it wouldn't—but all the risk was on the customer. The vendor got paid either way.

Not surprisingly, that kind of arrangement didn't last. And what replaced it was the idea of software as a service, where the product was sold as a subscription, which gave the buyer more leverage (since he could cancel along the way). If the product doesn't work as promised, the buyer cancels the subscription and stops paying.

Simultaneously, customer service as a core component of business strategy started coming to the fore worldwide. Until then, customer service was considered a *nice-to-have*, but few spent an inordinate amount of time thinking about how to make it more efficient or effective or, more importantly, how it could be a form of competitive advantage. Starting in the early 1990s, that changed. Creating *customers for life* became the new mantra.

There was nothing wrong with that—everyone likes to receive good service—but the idea quickly became corrupted, which, in turn, caused two sets of problems.

First, people decided that what customer service meant was that you had to satisfy your customers (i.e., you always had to give them what they wanted, whether it was in their best interests or not). Here's a simple example. Some companies decided on their own that what their customers wanted was for the phone to be answered in two rings or less when someone called seeking assistance. But a quick check with customers showed they would be willing to have the phone ring far longer if the person who finally picked up was able to help them the first time every time. That's what really mattered, not how fast the phone was answered.

> *Having something for everyone means there is not enough for anyone.*

The second problem is that clients aren't monolithic. Different people within a company have different wants and desires. And so, the problem with customer satisfaction is that you are constantly trying to cater to all of your individual clients' different shifting appetites at once, rather than concentrating on what will truly make the client's company successful.

That brings us back to software as a service and its inherent limits. While it is certainly better than selling a product to customers who have little recourse, software as a service is still pretty similar to the situation we had before. Vendors are still selling software—although the sale is through a subscription. And on the other side of the table you have somebody buying something. True, they are buying a subscription, but the whole thing continues to feel transaction oriented.

And that is a problem. For the buyer-seller relationship to work, it needs to be a partnership. There needs to be a common vision of what both the buyer and the seller want to achieve, coupled with the feeling on both sides that, "If you don't succeed, I don't succeed."

> *As we said in chapter 1, in the future, every corporate purchaser will say, "You want me to buy your product or service? Fine. Here's the specific, quantifiable outcome I want. Prove to me that you are going to provide it, in collaboration with me, and I'll buy. If you can't, I won't."*

That thought led us to the concept of value as a service—the idea that the seller and buyer determine what will make the customer successful together, and then the vendor delivers that.

Simply put, the days of selling stuff that doesn't deliver are over.

SKIN IN THE GAME

Obviously, this is a different way to think about how to do business. But thinking differently won't take hold unless the behavior of everyone in your organization works to make it a reality.

> *It's one thing to say, "We're focused on customer success." It's quite another to ingrain that belief into a vibrant, effective company culture that delivers on the promise. Customer success requires both a laser focus and a pervasive, daily cultural attitude and enthusiasm.*

Take sales reps as one example. They need to be totally focused on their clients' long-term success, rather than on a front-end win. That's how we try to do business at our company. Our own sales reps don't push for the big sale up front, nor do they sell more features than a customer can successfully deploy. Every ounce of their energy, financing, and creative juice goes into how to make this sale a value as a service that everyone can agree with.

Again, why would a customer be willing to pay for anything that doesn't work or that they don't need? Our success is our customers' success; we have real skin in the game, and so do our customers on an ongoing basis. That's the only profitable, sustainable route going forward.

Do This Personally as Well

Let's stop and underscore a point we have made a couple of times throughout the book: You, personally, can (and should) deliver value as a service to advance your career.

The first step is determining what matters to your company.

Listen to what your supportive manager is saying about the priorities of your business. Think about what your CEO is saying about her strategy for the company and figure out how the things you are working on—or could be working on—can map into that. Understand what your CFO is trying to achieve over the next three to five years. Is it cost cutting? Is it compliance? Is it minimizing supplier risk? Is it having visibility into how the company is spending money? Is it growing revenue?

Once you know your business's definition of success, figure out how you can help make it happen. What are the things you can do that can deliver the most value? What are the best metrics to use? That way when someone comes to you with an idea or a project to work on, you can step back and ask, "But how will that get us to this particular corporate goal?"

You want to be known as a person who contributes to the company's success. Today, every company is—or soon will be—a knowledge-based company. One way you can prove you have the knowledge, skills, and abilities that companies need is by insisting on value as a service as part of everything you touch.

As we have seen throughout the book, you need to be able to quantify that success. For some companies it will be, "Because we hired this vendor, we are now able to expand 100 percent faster. It used to take us four months to get into a new market. Now it takes just two."

Others will say, thanks to buying from our new vendor, we have been able to reduce headcount by 20 percent.

But most of the time, the benefit of buying value as a service will be expressed in currency. As we saw in chapter 4, when some of Coupa's customers talked about how this works, they always quantified the savings. They talked about how much money they saved processing purchase orders more efficiently, how they were able to take advantage of discounts by paying early, how they reduced supplier overpayments by X, and so on.

Now, this underscores two important points.

First, there needs to be complete agreement on both sides as to what success should look like. As we saw in chapter 2, when we discussed the ineffective rollout of the Affordable Care Act's website and the problems the state of Florida had in trying to create its online marketplace, if the client is not clear on what they are trying to achieve, success is unlikely.

Similarly, as our experience with Subway (as we talked about in chapter 4) shows, if the vendor—in this case, it was us—can't help the client define success metrics, things are not going to go—or end—well.

The takeaway for both buyers and sellers is this: If you don't know exactly what success is going to look like when you're through, don't start.

The second point is that you need to build a value-creation culture—one that is unified around beliefs that everyone can rally around. In our case, they are ensuring customer success, focusing on results, and striving for excellence.

You need to reinforce those values by hiring and promoting people who exemplify these values and by disproportionately rewarding the ones who execute them on an extraordinary basis.

A value-creation culture cannot be ordered from on high. The values need to resonate with your employees, who need to make them their own. The values need to be simple, clear, and constantly reinforced, which is something I cannot stress enough. Otherwise, they will never take hold.

How do you know they have taken hold? When you see people modeling the behaviors you want and isolating those who don't support the company's way of doing things.

YOU CAN DO THIS

This book has been about sharing best practices (i.e., what has worked well for other firms as well as what has been successful for our customers and for us).

What we have found is that our best deployments have been the ones where we have clearly articulated up front:

▶ How we will measure success

▶ Whether there is a crucial level of adoption

▶ What the impact to operating expenses will be

▶ If there is a certain result set that can be mapped to profitability, actual shareholder value, or an uptick in stock price

We then match the deployment—our action plan—against the objectives. That's what keeps everybody focused on what is essential to creating success.

> **Success requires accountability on both sides.**

Let's run through a series of examples.

Maybe the client has a solid core business, and the CEO wants to drive profitability. So on the procurement side, their entire initiative should be about cost reduction—period.

Maybe the company is growing quickly, but they have no idea if they're spending money wisely. We might focus on getting visibility into all methods of spend by category, as quickly as possible, so they can make the most strategic decisions on spending money.

Maybe a client company has minimal compliance, and they're worried about government audits, or they're concerned that their culture is great but there aren't many controls. In this case, we'll focus everything on compliance to get them within the restrictions within a certain period of time.

Maybe the goal is increasing shareholder value.

Or maybe they simply want the process to be much more efficient so everyone can get home by dinnertime. The possibilities are endless.

There are dozens of ways to create value. The point is, once you get customer success in your sights, you should never lose your aim. That business objective—achieving success—is first, and everything else comes second. There are a great many things that matter in life, but when it comes to your business, all that matters is the success of your clients.

START TODAY

Now is the time to move to value as a service for four reasons.

First, customers are going to demand it. To use two clichés, which became clichés because they are true: The world is flat, and it is also transparent. Because the world is flat, your customers are aware of best practices that exist anywhere around the globe. They know who is providing value as a service (and who isn't). And if they aren't sure, it doesn't take them long to learn the answer. Since the world is transparent—thanks to the web—they can find out fairly quickly. There is no place to hide. As we said in chapter 6, you used to be able to sell on the sizzle. Now, customers are demanding the steak at all times.

Second, there is a huge first-mover advantage. Damon Runyon, the writer whose street-smart New York characters gave us *Guys and Dolls* and countless short stories, had an expression that he used a lot: "The race does not always go to the swift, nor the battle to the strong—but that's the way to bet." You want to make the move to providing value as a service now, or you risk being left behind.

Third, change takes time. Altering the way you do business does not happen overnight, and the bigger your company, the more time it takes. That's the most practical reason for starting the transition now.

The fourth reason is that change is hard. The natural inclination, as we talked about earlier in the book, is to put it off until it is absolutely required. Don't.

By the time you decide you are ready to change, you may have already lost the game. Your competition may have transformed the landscape, and you may have been disrupted to the point where your product or service has become a commodity—or worse.

But as you make the move, you will have to think differently.

Before, you were focused on delivering a good product or a reliable service—meeting deadlines, turning a profit, and the like. All those things are still important. But they have moved down a notch—or soon will—on your priority list. At the top, as we have seen, needs to be making sure your customer is successful.

What follows is that you need to reassess the way you market, what you believe your core competencies are, your culture, and everything that's going on in terms of your organization to make sure you are concentrating on your customer's success.

What that means, of course, is that you will need to reevaluate how you evaluate everything.

You will not necessarily have to look for new metrics (although you might). It's that you will look at existing metrics in new ways. For example, as we talked about in chapter 7, investors and board members want to see that a company is investing sufficiently in sales and marketing. But if they see those costs are extremely high, and the company is extremely unprofitable, they will have serious concerns.

However, going forward, if that company is able to clearly articulate how they're creating undeniable value for their customers, and the firm's reputation is growing, there will be far greater confidence. The classic example of that, as we saw in chapter 7, was Amazon, which spent a fortune, but they eventually became one of the first choices when it comes to buying something online.

What the Amazon example shows is that the definition of success may change in the future as well. Today, it could be having the greatest net margins. Tomorrow, it could be how many profitable revenue-sharing ventures you have with your clients.

We aren't sure exactly what all the new success models will look like, but we are certain they will all revolve around providing value as a service.

DID WE DELIVER VALUE?

O bviously, I hope you enjoyed the book. More importantly, I hope it provided ideas that can help you and your company transition to providing value as a service and becoming more successful.

That was the idea behind the project, and we should be judged by how well we did that. But how exactly should we be judged? Well, it makes sense to hold us to our own standards.

> *As we have said throughout, for a project to be successful, the vendor and the client need to agree on what value is. Then, the vendor needs to hit agreed-upon metrics for providing it.*

Well, in the case of this book, we are the vendor. And though we haven't been able to engage with you in a one-on-one conversation about what would constitute value, we probably can take a guess: providing information that could help you, and your company, perform better.

But how much information? (This book is all about quantifying success, after all.)

Well, one of the ways you can agree on value, as we talked about in chapter 2, is to benchmark.

And so we did.

James Walker Michaels, the long-time editor of *Forbes*, ran the magazine for thirty-seven years and is recognized as the person who created business journalism as we now know it. He used to tell his writers if the magazine delivered just one article per issue that a reader found useful, the reader would renew for life.

Forbes' continuing success proved he was right.

Well, books are longer than magazines, and they cost more, so we needed to extrapolate from Michaels's comment. A quick check with a handful of business book editors and writers made it clear that, for most readers, three worthwhile ideas justify the investment of time and money in a book.

That is the standard we want to be held against.

Did we deliver three worthwhile ideas that can improve your business or your career?

Please let me know at Rob@Coupa.com.

Thank you.

ACKNOWLEDGMENTS

Special thanks to the Coupa team:

Ameet Prabhu Salgaonkar	Sal Alswafta	Lambert Nguyen
Anthony Tiscornia	Terri Taylor	Lei Pan
Brannon Adlesh	Todd Ford	Natalie Cedeno
Ciara Winston	Tyler Chamberlain	Raymond Martinelli
David Irwin	Victoria Alvarez	Larry Sanford
Dusti Singleton	William McPartlon Jr.	Lauren Rhodes
J Dexter Ramsey	Atish Singh	Leah Moore
Jessica Murillo	Daniel Ricardez	Luke Leonard
Justin Stern	Roneel Prasad	Mikayla Kirkpatrick
Mario Ibarra	Jonathan Stueve	Natalie Wilson
Matthew Lawrence	Karen Piry	Owen Murray
Maurizio Baratta	Linh Dieu	Sandy McGregor
Robin Turner	Aidan O'Neill	Stephanie Sherwood
Roger Kopfmann	Donna Li	Tracy Billups

Valentina Berry

Adrianna Tozzi

Alicia Haag

Brenda Terschuren

Michele McDowall

Virginia Synnott

Alexander Kleiner

Junaid Mohiuddin

Robert Bernshteyn

Brenton Lyon

Catherine
    Perry-Robertson

David Shanteler

David Wolstencroft

James Dinette

Joseph Freitag

Kevin Farrell

Philippe Martinez

Roger Goulart

Rusty Nail

Sally Stephens

Shankar VR

Yongdok Kang

Alan Ortiz

Alberto Ciaramella

Andrew Turner

Clinton Pohler

Colin Fisk

Daniel Adrian

David Hall

Edmund Pritchard

Elizabeth Simpson

Farzad Wahab

Gabriele Buffarini

Grant Thorburn

Itamar Correia

Jake Sells

James Shreckengost

Jason Atkins

Jayde Look

Jeffrey Lo

Jenny Lee

Jose Rodriguez

Jose Maria Garcia

Julius Kvedaras

Kieran Brady

Kristien Templin

Kristine Barats

Le Liu

Louis Bizouerne

Mangesh Pohekar

Marc Christoph

Matthew Wint

Mauricio Marroquin

Mayuresh Thakur

Michael Baldwin

Michael Weir

Michael Hsu

Michael O'Grady

Michael McNulty

Michelle Luckie

Milind Powar

Nancy Abraham

Nathalie Otala

Patrick Collins

Philipp Gieschen

Rakesh Tatineni

Sarah Boyne

Satish Satalluri

Sharon Galler

Silvia Sirbu

Sonali Thakur

Stefano Tagliabue

Subhasish Sarkar

Swapnil Arora

Swapnil Khare

Timothy Methenitis

Tuyen Huynh

Wendy Gold

Zaki Fall

Amit Utreja

Ashley Dale

Charchit Arora

Charles Cooke

Edward Lucero

Hans Gustavson

Jaldhi Valia

Acknowledgments

Miroslaw Baran

Miroslaw Jaworski

Philip Cox

Pierluigi Riti

Ricardo Aravena

Sanket Naik

Ben Parker

Emeka Ejiofor

Harvey Brauner

James Simmons

Julian Peebles

Julie Prochasson-Restrepo

Scott Cohen

Steve Taylor Jr.

Allison Reid

Andreas Schroth

Aneet Kohli

Anthony Rich

Barbara Tygesen

Benjamin Mlynash

Carl Nyquist

Craig Yee

Daniella Stanghellini

Declan Fanning

Douglas Duker

Eleanore Dogan

Elisabeth Magnee-Schalch

Emma Curran

Eric Schrader

Eugenie Garnier

Gregory Setser

Imreet Bhatia

Jason Braun

Jean-David Faure

Jerome Josserand

Jonathan Fear

Jonathan Chaplin

Kandharuben Govender

Kavalinder Randhawa

Krystal Hunt

Martin Hayles

Maura Zeph

Maurice Wells

Max Mishka

Meredith Blake

Michael Brady

Narayanan Beegamudre

Navin Vardya

Osprey Brown

Pamela McClure-Roman

Paul Coviello

Per Andersson

Pritesh Patel

Ralph Schermann

Ravi Thakur

Raymond Whiteside Jr.

Richard Anderson

Simon Kelly

Stephan Herrel

Susan Hans

Thomas Speich

Tommaso Susini

Venkat Tummalapalli

William Whitten

Adam Rhine

Adam Alphin

Ajmel Kottai

Alastair Bennett

Andrew Miller

Avijit Mukherji

David Uriarte

Faraz Qureshi

Ian McNelly

Mary Anne Krzeminski

Olivier Duval

Phannga Pathammavong

Rajiv Ramachandran

Rebecca Smyth

Rohit Jalisatgi

Ronney Kandah

Sabaji Naik

Thomas Knott

Trishanth Vallurupalli

Alexis Hartmann

Amy Ingham

Andy Lightfoot

Benjamin Marini

Carl Warwick

Catherine Cowley

Cesar Montero Garcia

Chai Loong Tan

Charles Brunson

Christine LaScola

Craig Bittner

Daria Ghiassi

David Hasegawa

David Hosford

David Motta

Gary Holland

Glenn Billqvist

Gustaf Tanate

James McParlane

Jean Francois Dall'Aglio

Jeffery Novak

Jennifer Schmidt

John Mattinson

John Zimmerman

Jonathan Porta Perez
    Martin

Karen Richter

Karsten Rose

Kevin Clark

Lance Olson

Lyndon Teoh

Madeline Maldonado

Magnus Ljung

Marc Langer

Marco Sa

Mark McCarthy

Martin Leahy

Martyn Craven

Milos Lekovic

Neil Mahimker

Neil Barton

Nicholas Picone

Olivier Chalon

Philippe Delebarre

Rene Appeldorn

Robert Cornelius

Robert Thoms

Robert Glenn

Roman Moreno

Scott Rowland

Sean Simpson

Steven Daly

Terri Hayslip

Thomas Rogers

Thomas Tanetschek

Timothy Hamilton

Walter Sharp

Warwick Henderson

William Patzer

William McMullen

William Bowen

William Nutter

William Goodall

Brian Seiler

Brian Motsett

Bruno Sireyjol

Camille Falor

Christopher Noseworthy

Craig Dawkins

David Chambers

Eric Brown

Filip Morael-Poniatowski

Gilles Declercq

Gregory Loomis

James Hegerich

Jason Handley

Jonathan Nye

Joseph Alvarez

Joseph Larkins

Kannitha Garcia

Klaus Tenderich

Louis Braun

Mark Baemmert

Mary Flynn Barton

Nicholas Elhini

Randall Briggs

Robert Whitcher

Stephen Cleminson

Suzanne Akins

Terry Ayers

Thomas Grimes

Acknowledgments

Will Martoni	Christopher Hahn	Brian Waller
William Atkins	Christopher Radding	Ellie Wu
Albert Tommei	David Nuno Heredia	Franck Quetier
Bruce Gagnard	Debbie Kirkwood	James Turner
Craig DeMartini	Derrick Leck	Ken Eales
Daniel Tarver	Frank Cappel	Kevin Rucker
David Eyres	Jean-Marc Quenet	Kevin Mueller
Hakan Duran	Jeremy Aubert	Kim Dickson
James Plato	Jonathan Goss	Leslie Pollak
Jonathan Weiss	Jonathon Siudut	Lori Yonelunas
Jure Ljubicic	Joseph Larko	Yasmir Williams
Jutta von Ebbe	Kendra Von Esh	Amit Duvedi
Lilia Boslo	Louis Wong	Craig Suyematsu
Lisa Elie	Mark McKinlay	David Hearn
Mark Davoren	Matthew Andrews	Jeffery Collins
Mellyna Romo	Michael Conway	Joe Robertson
Pearly Jadin	Nigel Henshaw	Kalim Khan
Richard Blackburn	Olivier Bilger	Lisa Daly
Richard Chapman	Paul Stuker	Michael Chu
Sofia Arroyo	Peter DiFalco	Michal Wolosz
Stephane Renard	Phil Foti	Raul Villarreal Jr.
Steven Avila	Phillip Hamilton	Richard Witt
Wynn Belton	Pierre-Andre Sinoir	Robert Jan Vissers
Allan Fish	Raymond Pell	Sanjayan Manivannan
Anita Carew	Rob Rousou	Stephen Woo
Asif Bhanwadia	Ronan Kerouedan	Thomas Aitchison
Brandon Henderson	Simon Hurst	Tiffanie Brown Craig
Chandra Rao	Stephen Will	Aaron McIntyre
Chris Turner	Aaron Wargo	Abdul Chaudhry

Aditya Mandavilli

Ajoy Satheesh

Amit Suryavanshi

Amy MacKinnon

Anand Ramakrishnan

Anshuman Nene

Ashish Saihgal

Asokumar Shanmugam

Bing-Chang Lai

Bradley Rosintoski

Brendan Mulholland

Brent Wooden

Brian Farr

Bryan Kaplan

Chethan Visweswar

Christopher Fung

Christopher Lanier

Christopher Mayor

Curtis Moore

Dan Dimerman

Daniel Chan

David Lee

Debanjan Sengupta

Deepthi Somasunder

Dexter Vu

Dmitri Korobov

Dmytro Landberg

Gireesh Malaksamudra

Hanieh Borhanazad

Hardik Joshi

Harsha Bhat

Hunpin Toh

Jayakanthan Selvaraj

Jayaprakash
  Krishnamoorthy

Jeffrey Hellman

Jimmy Chandra

Johan Wu

Keeyoung Kim

Kent Mewhort

Ketan Darji

Kevin Old

Khee Wong

Kusno Mudiarto

Luke Hammond

Maurice Fitzgerald

Michael Wagner

Morteza Madadi

Mykhailo Liubarskyi

Neha Gujar

Noriaki Hamamoto

Oleksandr Mekhovov

Omar Sehgal

Paul Collett

Raghavan Eachampadi

Rebecca Mengell

Robert Monahon

Robert Hernandez

Ryan Zhou

Sandeep Singarapu

Sandeep Kulkarni

Saravanapavan
  Jeyaramanan

Scott Yu

Si Li

Siavash Nikobonyadrad

Srinivasarao Konakanchi

Stephane Pelchat

Stephen Aghaulor

Steven Gravitz

Tejal Sanghvi

Thiago Jackiw

Thuwaragan
  Sundaramoorthy

Toru Mori

Tushar Rawal

Varun Gore

Vikas Panwar

Yao Yao

Yutaka Hosoai

Zachary Randles

Aldo Kurnia

Amar Ramdhave

Anand Chavan

Aparajita Shinde

Asha Naidu

Darryl Hunt

Acknowledgments

David Larsen	Anju Gupta	Timothy Durkin
Gregory Helmich	Carl Rydbeck	Ashish Deshpande
Harish Reddy Reddy	Christopher Yin	Mark Emmenegger
Jose Agustin Avila Perez	Cym Sanguinet	Penelope Foster
Kevin Chu	Daniel Mark	Timothy Schneider
Lakhan Pasari	David Jorgensen	Amy Wall
Martin Lienhard	Donna Wilczek	Ariadni Pereira
Masoud Mozayeni	Elliot Beaudoin	Cara Sivara
Matthew Otzwirk	Ethan Laub	Carolina Hoogeveen
Neetal Sharma	Iniobong Uto-Uko	Chien Liao
Peter Trice	James Laframboise	Gabriel Perez
Pooja Mangla	John Adger	Jessie Womble
Prabakaran Subramanian	Justin Mehta	Marisela Parra
Prakash Borkar	Kira Letskina	Neal Amsden
Priya Gopinath	Laverne Henderson	Nicole Romoli
Ramesh Sencha	Maggie Joy	Orlando DeBruce
Samata Yarlagadda	Mark Burch	Shruti Gokhale
Sangeetha Venkatraman	Markus Hornburg	Tara Ryan
Saurabh Shinde	Martin Ertl	
Sivapriya Ramachandran	Mikin Faldu	
Smita Ranade	Neha Arora	
Somnath Bhattacharjee	Pallavi Mathane	
Sunil Bolina	Parvez Syed	
Vilas Madapurmath	Rahul Mehta	
David Williams	Raja Hammoud	
Eddy Kim	Ramakrishnan Balaji	
Matthew Pasquini	Scott Harris	
Parand Darugar	Sricharan Iyengar	
Andrew Chiang	Stephen Cussen	

ABOUT THE AUTHOR

Rob is the chief executive officer and president of Coupa, and he drives the company's strategy and execution. He is the chairman of the Coupa board of directors. Since 2009, Rob has led Coupa to an over-100-percent compounded annual revenue growth and over-95-percent customer renewal rate. Rob has over two decades' experience in the business software industry. He came to Coupa from SuccessFactors, where he ran global product marketing and management as a member of the executive management team as the company scaled from an early start-up to a successful public company. Prior to that, Rob directed product management at Siebel Systems, where he helped build Siebel ERM into one of the company's fastest-growing product lines. Rob also did a stint in management consulting at McKinsey & Company, and he spent four years at Accenture, where he focused on global SAP systems implementations.

Rob is a guest lecturer at Harvard and Stanford business schools and a frequent contributor to *Forbes* and *Fortune* magazines. He can often be heard providing commentary on major news programs, including Bloomberg's *Money Moves* and NPR's *Morning Edition*. Rob holds a BS in information systems from the State University of New York at Albany and an MBA from Harvard Business School.

www.ValueAsService.com